"I have read 'Oil of Joy Instead of Mourning' with great interest. This is a program that has really touched my heart. To most of us these women are truly out-of-sight and out-of-mind and Rhonda Arias has opened a door for us to know them. She is to be warmly commended for her loving effort." J. C. Wilke, M.D., president of Life Issues Institute, Cincinnati, OH, and author of "Why Can't We Love Them Both: Questions and Answers About Abortion".

"Women are often pushed or even forced into unwanted abortions. Whether the result of coercion or free choice, any abortion can traumatize a woman's life and lead to substance abuse and other self-destructive behaviors. A high proportion of women in prison are victims of unwanted, unsafe abortions which intensified or complicated prior problems and often create new emotional and behavioral problems. The emotional and spiritual needs of these imprisoned women are often forgotten and neglected. Rhonda Arias has been on the forefront of bringing post-abortion ministry to these incarcerated women for over ten years. Now she is sharing her experiences and insights in 'Oil of Joy Instead of Mourning'. I am confident that it will be an invaluable resource for anyone seeking to minister to the broken hearts, and often abused spirits, in our prisons." David C. Reardon, Ph.D., president of the Elliott Institute, Springfield, IL, and author of "Making Abortion Rare".

"With this offering Rhonda Arias makes an important contribution to the sphere of abortion recovery ministry. Her years of experience in the field are skillfully brought to the pages of this dynamic work. This book is sure to have a dramatic and powerful impact on those women dealing with post-abortive issues. It will also serve as a surefire guide for those counselors, pastors, or clinicians desiring to work in this challenging area of ministry. This book is a needed addition to the therapeutic literature and will benefit anyone dealing with issues of abortion and its aftermath." David Rodriguez, D.Min., BCBT, CPC, President of Therapon Institute for Biblical counseling, and senior pastor of Christian Fellowship, Marrero, LA

"Wake up America, and realize that there is a war going on for the seed of the woman. We've got something inside of us that is bigger than the children that we lost. The battle that we are in now is for our children, but also for the soul of the woman. Rhonda's book resurrects the soul of the woman who's had her motherhood stolen through abortion. It's about more than recovery; it's about restoration of the family". Carol Everrett, ceo of The Heidi Group, Round Rock, TX, and author of "Blood Money: Getting Rich Off A Woman's Right To Choose".

Oil of Joy
Instead of Mourning

Oil of Joy
Instead of Mourning

Restoring the joy of motherhood after the grief of abortion

Rhonda Arias

ISBN 978-0-557-58135-1

Specialized training in therapy methods is highly recommended for facilitators of this curriculum and can be obtained by contacting www.oilofjoyformourning.org.

A comprehensive Bible study for incarcerated women for healing from abortion and other sexual sin and abuse.

To Jessica, Jacquilyn, and Joanna,

who taught me the tenacity of God's love,
gave me reason to love again,
and filled my life with joy!

Acknowledgements

Jesus is the vine and I am the branch. He is the vinedresser who loves His vineyard. Without Him there would be no love in me to remember the prisoners, and no wisdom to set them free. He is the aleph and the tav, the beginning and the end of every work that remains. All my love is due Him.

Over one hundred **volunteers** throughout the state of Texas have given their hearts and their time to remember the prisoners in ten years of Oil of Joy outreaches. They have broken the covenant of death made through abortion, enforced the covenant of life through His blood, and written this text with their sweat and many tears.

I want to thank the Gideon's army of **prophetic intercessors** who understood the spiritual battle, and waged war on behalf of me, my family, and the volunteers who entered the enemy's camp to set women free. These intercessors would not ask that their names be written here, but their names are known in heaven.

I will ever be indebted to **Jerry Groom**, then head of TDC chaplaincy, now pastor of First Assembly of God, Kaufman, TX, who took my trembling hand and prayed the dangerous prayer with me to ask God if He really wanted me to go into prisons with abortion recovery. Then Jerry became the Christ-like mediator between me and the prison system, and the doors were opened to our ministry teams.

Many **chaplains** within the Texas Dept. of Criminal Justice have inspired us to do our best, and encouraged us to keep doing what no one else in prison ministry was doing. Chaplain Gloria Siller was the first to make Oil of Joy a part of her unit's programming. She understood the grief of a mother who misses a child she never held, and did not overlook the need for abortion recovery. She inspired us to also be good Samaritans who do not walk by and leave someone in a ditch of forgetfulness, but to remember the post-abortive women in prison. David Lopez always stood with us and acted as a father who makes a way in TDCJ. Without Chaplain Sandy Biles, our ministry teams would not be the well-oiled machine that they are today. My heartfelt appreciation goes out to this mentor in the faith who has helped us know how to be a helper to chaplains.

I want to thank Texas **Governor Rick Perry**, who listened with great interest about what God was doing in Texas women's prisons to restore women after abortion, and who understood that true rehabilitation of women was not possible without abortion recovery as part of the programming in the criminal justice system. I am thankful for a governor who knows God, who understands the power of redemption, and who did exactly what he told me he would do to create open doors in the system.

Remember the prisoners, as though chained with them. since you are in the body also. Hebrews 13:3

Contents

Introduction

In 1973 the highest court of the U.S. passed down a decision that would socially engineer a culture of death. The media campaign that drove popular opinion was called 'choice'. Our society had overridden the honorable call of motherhood with the worship of individualism.

Under the guise of 'choice', a mother's decision to abort her unborn child was put on the same moral plane as a decision to carry that life to term, based solely on the welfare of the woman. Ostensibly, women are given this choice so that they can have greater control over their future. Women who choose abortion are painted as smart decision-makers who are focused on achievement and success, and will not allow an unplanned pregnancy to stand in their way. In my ten years of work in the rehabilitation of women in Texas prisons, I have found multitudes of women whose ability to set and achieve goals was severely hindered by an abortion decision. I have yet to meet one who achieved a high level of success after abortion, and most have difficulty even starting and finishing a single task.

To Ashley[1] the abortion decision was the result of what felt like a life-or-death crisis. She felt that her own life was at stake. She opted for saving her lifestyle only to see herself as a selfish unworthy mother for the rest of her life. Never again would she trust her ability to make good decisions. Since she was bound to fail, why even try? Ashley[1] has not been empowered by 'choice'.

Individual fulfillment is achieved in the context of each person's relationship to the community. That community begins with the family. It is never in the interest of a mother to end her relationship with her unborn child. Motherhood is the garden where selfless contributions are planted for the good of greater community. It is where a mother learns to give freely and love unconditionally. Through mothering, women learn to sow into purpose that is greater than them, thus finding their own individual fulfillment. It is in a mother's interest to nurture her relationship with her offspring because life begets life, and one does reap what one sows.

To some, abortion was sold as the way to escape subjugation by males. Women didn't want to become 'baby machines', pregnant at the whim of an insecure male who sees his prowess exemplified by how many women bear his children. The truth is that the decision is not always made by the pregnant mother. Some were forced by parents under financial pressure, others by pimps driven by their own lust for power and money. In working with incarcerated women who regret their abortions, we have found more women were coerced through means ranging from psychological warfare to physical threats, beatings, and other violence, than who actually chose abortion because it seemed the right thing to do to them. They did not see themselves as free-thinking, take-charge women; but as women trapped without a choice. The very thing that was supposed to free them from male dominion became the means by which they were oppressed and abused.

You can ask Rachel[1], who is serving 25 years in a Texas prison for domestic violence that led to murder. Her husband's death was the result of her rage after he forced her to abort their second child. Death begets death.

Abortion did not make women more free. The rate of incarceration showed a sharp increase in the U.S. after the legalization of abortion in 1973[2], and the rate of incarceration among women is increasing more rapidly among women than among men[3]. Though scientific studies showing a causal relationship between abortion and incarceration of women are yet to be done, over 60% of women in Oil of Joy surveys in prisons say that their abortion was the pivotal point where their anti-social behaviors began which eventually led them to prison[4].

There are many scientific studies showing a causal relationship between abortion and substance abuse[5]. Ask any prison chaplain what effect drugs and alcohol abuse have on the rate of incarceration. Better yet, ask the women themselves. We asked the women in our abortion recovery programs in the state of Texas what part their abortion played in their substance abuse, and just over 83% of them said that substance abuse either started or sharply increased immediately following their abortion[6].

By their own testimony, abortion also caused depression in these women (63percent) and disruption of interpersonal relationships (63.5percent)[4]. Many women felt a strange detachment from their other children once an abortion had taken place in their lives, and their inability to bond with their child, coupled with their depression and anger problems, caused difficulty in successful parenting. Decisions were made with disregard for their children's security; yet what women think about most while they are locked up is their children. With time on their hands, they start to meditate on what went wrong, and they remember their abortions. Once again they start to rethink the decisions that were made along the path to the abortion clinic's doors. Those who search for truth in humility are transformed from victimized girls without understanding to victorious mothers who leave a legacy of life.

Citations

1. The sanctity of human life is to be celebrated in its utmost through respect for each person's unique contribution to the community. In honor of the brave women who have decided in the midst of their incarceration to become responsible for each other's healing by sharing openly, and once again find their worth and dignity through the nurture of a micro-community of small group therapy, I site their cases with their names changed to protect their right to confidentiality.

2. U.S. Dept. of Justice, Bureau of Justice Statistics, Table 6.22 at http://www.albany.edu/sourcebook/pdf/1622/pdf.

3. U.S. Department of Justice, Bureau of Justice Statistics reveal that the number of women under th jurisdiction of State or Federal prison authorities increased 4.9% during 2002, while the number of men rose just 2.4%. Bureau of Justice Statistics, U.S. Dept. of Justice, Prisoners in 2002 (July 2003 & March 2004). In another study researchers found that female patients were likely to have experienced an abortion in the same year as their alcohol related problems began. E.R. Morrissey, et al., "Stressful Life Events and Alcohol Problems Among Women seen at a Detoxification Center," J. Studies on Alcohol, 39(9)1559, 1978.

4. Oil of Joy Program surveys and evaluations, 2004, affidavit submitted to the Supreme Court of the United States, amicus brief No. 04-967.

5. During in depth interviews with post-abortion women, the majority of specifically attributed their drug or alcohol abuse to stress related to the abortion. Only 10% stated they had already engaged in substance abuse prior to their abortions. A. Speckhard, Psycho-Social Stress Following Abortion, Ph.D. Thesis, University of Minnesota, 1985

6. Oil of Joy Program surveys and evaluations, 2005- 2009 received from 1,693 post-abortive women in prison.

Program Overview

This book is to be used as a curriculum guide for incarcerated women, and is only one of the tools in a comprehensive program of abortion recovery designed by Oil of Joy. Each offender's healing will be in direct proportion to the degree that she applies herself to completing this Bible study and participating in the small group and corporate exercises.

Typically, the program is introduced to the prison population through church services. Registration is achieved through intake forms given at the service, and is left open to the general population until the second week of the program. Due to the intimate and personal nature of discussion, attendance is closed by the third week of a 10-week program.

The first step in each offender's healing is completing an Oil of Joy intake form. This is a self-evaluation that will help women identify how their abortion has affected them. Certain sociodemographic and personal history characteristics are noted and considered before approval to the program. Skilled facilitators will guide the healing process accordingly, applying various methods of therapy at each stage of the healing process. The intake will also be used as a measure for evaluation once the program is completed.

Worship and thankful remembering is an important part of the rehabilitation program. The program also consists of weekly teaching by a ministry leader, followed by small group therapy. Facilitators for the small groups are not teachers, but lay-counselors trained to recognize and facilitate each task area of healing. They act as leader-guides for each woman's journey of self-discovery, and as watchmen for sound doctrinal foundation.

Therapeutic methods include active listening, giving and receiving feedback from other participants in the small group, healing memories through prayer, question and answer series for cognitive decision-making, and tactile interactive object-lesson exercises. Closure to the loss of the child is achieved through a memorial service for the unborn.

Effectiveness is tracked through a comparative analysis using exit surveys to determine which of the symptoms stated on the intake has abated, and in some cases, to what degree. Recommendations for continued rehabilitation are made, and each woman states her progress and plans at the graduation ceremony.

Joy Instead of Mourning

Session 1

To comfort all who mourn, to console those who mourn in Zion,
To give them beauty for ashes, the oil of joy for those who mourn.
Isaiah 61: 2b, 3a

This study is about the journey to joy that starts with permission to mourn. Mourning is an expression of grief and sorrow. Grief comes from loss. Abortion is a loss of something very precious and dear to a mother - her child. Processing the grief from abortion is often difficult because we live in a world that does not recognize abortion as a child loss. The kingdoms of this world have sanctioned abortion as a reproductive health choice. Yet we find it was neither reproductive, nor healthy.

The Truth Will Set You Free

It is healthy to grieve abortion for what it is. Prolonged or deterred grief can hinder you emotionally, and keep you from making good choices now and in the future. Carrying the grief of a past abortion will end up stealing your destiny. Healthy grieving heals emotions and restores confidence so that you can move forward in life making courageous choices.

A decision to grieve an abortion is a search for God's heart and His redemptive purpose. We are embarking on a spiritual journey that includes looking back and remembering events from God's perspective. When the loss is processed through the eyes of God, truth is revealed. When truth is revealed, we are free to choose wisely.[1]

Getting God's perspective is like seeing into His Kingdom. This is not possible without a personal relationship with Him. In the gospel of John, chapter 3, verse 3, Jesus said that unless one is born again, he cannot see into the Kingdom of God. To be born again means that the life of your spirit is renewed with the Spirit of the Life-Giver. It is a supernatural experience that creates communion with God. Your destiny is within His Kingdom, but you must enter in.

Jesus asked people to repent, because the Kingdom of God was near (Matthew 3:2, 4:17). Repentance is not just turning from what you've been *doing*, but turning from the way you've been *thinking*. Jesus actually asks us to change the way we were thinking about abortion. He invites us to see our choices from His perspective. God's perspective gives us eyes to see the truth.

Jesus is the way, the truth, and the life. No one comes into the Kingdom of His Father except through Him. Are you willing to be born again, so that you can see into the Kingdom? Recapture your life and destiny now by coming to Him. He's been waiting for you. Stop and just speak to Him now if you are willing. You may want to write your prayer here.

Free Indeed[1]

If you are reading this from inside the walls of a prison or jail, then abortion is not the only loss you are grieving. You have temporarily lost your freedom.

God designed freedom. He created human beings with a free will. God gave us freedom because He values us. He honored us with the ability to make a choice to love Him. He is not out to control us; He is out to love us. He is after your heart.

In the beginning, Adam and Eve were free to enjoy the garden. They were sharing with God's dominion of the earth by tending and keeping it. God's blessing was upon them. Their choices were limited by only one tree. When they chose to eat the fruit of that tree, they didn't gain anything, but they greatly limited their freedom, and incurred great loss. Then they became enslaved to the earth, instead of having dominion over it.[2]

Freedom of choice, used irresponsibly, brings bondage into our lives. Every bad choice we make lessens our freedom until eventually; we may find ourselves behind bars with no rights, no privileges, and very few choices. If you are thinking that God wanted you incarcerated, think again. God hates bondage. Choices outside of God's design cause suffering and loss. The Bible says you have been called to liberty.[3]

Can you imagine God behind bars? 2 Corinthians 3:17 says that where the Spirit of the Lord is, there is liberty. Can you imagine anything so powerful that it would overcome Him and lock Him up? So when we find ourselves behind bars with most of our choices taken away, it is usually because we began making some choices along the way that separated us from Him. When choices are not in agreement with God's heart and generous Spirit, it causes loss after loss after loss. Perhaps the biggest loss is our ability to be close to God.

This study is about recognizing what our choices have cost us, and changing our hearts. It's about falling in love with God again, and learning to love what He loves and hate what He hates.[4]

Genesis records that when God made humans He breathed into His creation the breath of life. Isaiah records that every man's spirit is a direct gift from the Creator. God formed you, breathed His breath of life into you; then He blessed you. His design is life and blessings for us.

Choose Life

When we choose abortion, we are choosing to end a life. We are choosing death. God's beautiful words of instruction in the book of Deuteronomy reveal His heart pleading for our free will to be aligned with His will.

I call heaven and earth as witnesses today against you, that I have set before you life and death, blessing and cursing; therefore choose life, that both you and your descendants may live; Deut. 30:19

This study will also involve looking at how others have been affected by our choices. Adam and Eve's choice did not just affect them. It brought the curse of sin and death to the whole world.

I remember when I first told the story of creation and the fall of man to my children. I explained how much God wanted to bless us when He created us in the garden. Yet, Eve chose to eat of the forbidden fruit. My little girl looked up and said, "Oh Mommy, I wish she hadn't done that!" Her heart felt the loss. She saw what happened to Adam and Eve, and she grieved for all of us. I saw in her face the sorrow of a child who'd been affected by someone else's choice. I think in that moment I felt what God feels for His children. The grief that abortion causes is the curse of death that affects subsequent generations. As a parent looking into face of a child that day, I got a glimpse of our Father's heart. He wants to comfort us with the truth. He wants to teach us the consequences of our actions so that we can be empowered to make better choices in the future. He wants to give us a testimony of life.

Only take heed to yourself, and diligently keep yourself, lest you forget the things your eyes have seen, and lest they depart from your heart all the days of your life. And teach them to your children and your grandchildren. Deuteronomy 4:9

The Old Testament is a series of lessons on how turning from the love of God can cause us to go into captivity. The history of Israel reveals what happens collectively to a people who turn from God. In Isaiah 61, the prophet was speaking to a nation whose choices were leading them right into the captivity of Babylon. Their God-given destiny was to have dominion of their own land, but their choices were making them slaves to another kingdom. Isaiah foretold the coming of the Messiah when he proclaimed liberty to the captives.[5]

Approximately 650 years later, Jesus stood in the synagogue and publicly read Isaiah's gospel message. It's recorded in Luke 4. When He had finished reading these words, He sat down. All eyes were fixed on Him when He said to them, "Today this Scripture is fulfilled in your hearing." This is Jesus' proclamation of life and liberty.

The Spirit of the Lord is upon Me, Because He has anointed Me to preach the gospel to the poor; He has sent Me to heal the brokenhearted, to proclaim liberty to the captives and recovery of sight to the blind, to set at liberty those who are oppressed; Luke 4:18

We've made choices that were in agreement with death and not life; but Jesus came to give us back our lives. Abortion is a detour off the path of life, but Jesus came to get us back on track. As you trust in Him, He will show you the way to turn from agreement with death to life.

The thief does not come except to steal, and to kill, and to destroy. I have come that they may have life, and that they may have it more abundantly.
John 10:10

Calling abortion a "right" blinds us to the life within our wombs, and causes us to agree with death. Those of us who chose abortion believed at least one of the two major lies about abortion: #1: "It's not a baby" and/or #2: "It's the best thing for me to do." These lies robbed us of our child, and still seek to steal our destiny. He has seen the loss that believing these lies caused; and He has come to restore us to our destiny. He has so highly valued you that He has pursued you right into this facility, and brought with Him His anointing to heal your broken heart and make you free again. He came to give you back your life!

Since that day in the garden, the daughters of Eve have been mourning the loss of their freedom. Through sin, we lose relationship and connectedness to God, our life source. Right now you are probably thinking of some of the losses in your life. Maybe you have lost your sense of value and self-worth. Maybe you have lost a sense of direction and purpose. Maybe you have lost your children through your incarceration, through drug use, through miscarriage, or through abortion. When Jesus fulfilled Isaiah's prophesy, He was remembering the pain of our losses. He came to heal our pain.

Choose Freedom

God has a special heart for the prisoner. The first proclamation of Isaiah 61 was liberty to the captives, and the opening of their prison. The second proclamation of Isaiah 61 is acceptance. No matter what you've done, God still accepts *you*. His love is unconditional and enduring. The Old Testament scripture includes the 'day of vengeance of our God'; but when Jesus quoted this passage in the New Testament, He omitted that part. Perhaps that was because He knew that He had come to appease the wrath of God through His sacrifice for our sin. The only vengeance to be taken is going to be on the devil, the enemy of your soul. God is fighting harder for you than you have ever fought anyone.

1 John 3:8 says that Jesus came to destroy the works of the devil. The vengeance of God is now turned toward the devil. His lies have been the oppressors of our souls. Through faith in Jesus, we are free of the curse of sin and death. We are free to return to the lover of our souls and to love Him with all of our heart without condemnation.

God also has a special heart for those who mourn. Any mother who has lost a child deserves a right to mourn, even if she is partially responsible for that loss. Isaiah lists four promises for those who mourn. Can you read the passage in Chapter 61, verses 1 through 3 again and name the promises of mourning?

1. ____________________ 3. ____________________

2. ____________________ 4. ____________________

Which of these promises would you most like to see Jesus fulfill?
Write a letter to Him now telling Him what you need.

When you signed up for this class, you filled out an intake form identifying some of the symptoms of abortion. Over the course of the next 10 weeks, you will gain the means to identify the ways that your abortion experience has changed you, and lead you on the path to full restoration.

In the Oil of Joy support group, we will be working through some specific task areas of healing from your abortion(s). When you finish this Biblical course, you will be able to apply the process to other life hurts and traumatic experiences. The result is total transformation.

However, you must first focus on completing your healing from abortion. Your group leaders and the other women in your group will work with you, but you must do the work. If you leave out a step in the process, your healing in this area will be incomplete, so be diligent to work through each step.

Therefore, my beloved, as you have always obeyed, not as in my presence only, but now much more in my absence, work out your own salvation with fear and trembling; Philippians 2:12

The Journey

The first day of class, you will identify your goals for the course. Think about how abortion has affected your life and where you'd like God to heal you. Be as specific as you can. We'll start our homework lessons by studying the scriptures to renew our trust in a loving God who came to save us and heal us.

Then, we'll look deeper into some of life's hurts. This is important, because prior events may have affected the way you were thinking at the time of the abortion. These two steps are designed to correct any wrong thinking about who God is, and about who you are. This will bring us to a desire to be more like our Creator.

Our healing must include looking at those who we feel have wronged us, where our angry feelings are rooted, and how the feelings are affecting our beliefs and our attitudes today. By understanding God's forgiveness for us, and extending that forgiveness to others, we'll resolve those hurt and angry feelings.

Finally, we'll honor the memory of our children who've been lost by abortion, and move on to the unrestrained destiny that God purposed for our lives. God has already designed and blessed your journey. Simply place your trust in Him, and take the first step.

Scriptures Referenced

1. ***John 8:32** "And you shall know the truth and the truth shall make you free."*
2. ***Genesis 1:27 "So God created man in His own image; in the image of God He created him; male and female He created them. 28 Then God blessed them, and God said to them, "Be fruitful and multiply; fill the earth and subdue it; 3:17, Then to Adam He said, "Because you have heeded the voice of your wife, and have eaten from the tree of which I commanded you, saying, 'You shall not eat of it': "Cursed is the ground for your sake; In toil you shall eat of it All the days of your life".***
3. ***Galatians 5:13 "For you, brethren, have been called to liberty; only do not use liberty as an opportunity for the flesh, but through love serve one another."***
4. ***Numbers 10:35 "So it was, whenever the ark set out, that Moses said: "Rise up, O Lord! Let Your enemies be scattered, And let those who hate You flee before You."***
5. ***Isaiah 61: 1 "The Spirit of the Lord God is upon Me, Because the Lord has anointed Me To preach good tidings to the poor; He has sent Me to heal the brokenhearted, To proclaim liberty to the captives, And the opening of the prison to those who are bound; 2 To proclaim the acceptable year of the Lord, And the day of vengeance of our God; To comfort all who mourn, 3 To console those who mourn in Zion, To give them beauty for ashes, The oil of joy for mourning, The garment of praise for the spirit of heaviness; That they may be called trees of righteousness, The planting of the Lord, that He may be glorified."***

God is Not a Man

Session 2

God is not a man, that He should lie, nor a son of man, that He should repent. Has He said, and will He not do? Or has He spoken, and will He not make it good? Numbers 23:19

In ancient pagan cultures the gods were thought of as petty and covetous. They were very insecure and manipulative. The prevailing view was that the gods were like men. Knowledge of the one true God, the Creator of all Life, was non-existent in that culture.

The peoples' understanding of God was limited to their experiences with power-hungry men who don't keep their promises. Until we have developed a personal relationship with our Maker, our view of Him is much like that. It is limited to versions of our experiences with men. God is not a man.

God is Love — Day 1

What is your best definition of love? Did you grow up as a little girl with a storybook view of love, expecting a romantic love to one day overtake you? Perhaps you grew up believing that there was no such thing as true love; only manipulation between two people seeking to get their needs met. Most likely, your view is somewhere in between. The apostle John said, "God is love".

**And we have known and believed the love that God has for us.
God is love, and he who abides in love abides in God, and God in him.
1 John 4:16**

Those who say they love us, yet only take from us are not practicing God's kind of love. What did God's love motivate Him to do?

**For God so loved the world that He gave His only begotten Son, that whoever believes in Him should not perish but have everlasting life.
John 3:16**

John writes in the first chapter of his gospel that the Word is God; and the Word became flesh, and dwelt among us. His Son is an incarnation of Him. Jesus is the Spirit of God with flesh on. When God sent His Son, it was actually Him. His love motivated Him to give Himself.

During my third pregnancy, I used to speak to my baby in the womb. I was so elated that I was going to have someone to love. I used to tell my child that I loved him, and couldn't wait to play with him. I really wanted my child. But I didn't really love him. One day in the fourth month of the pregnancy, the circumstances of my life seemed to overwhelm me. I called the doctor who had been providing prenatal care and told him I had changed my mind. My life got in the way of my child's' life. I wasn't willing to give my life to him. I didn't have the kind of love that gives. I didn't have God's love.

Most mothers 'love' their children. But our love is not as pure or unfailing as God's love. Fears overtake us and we may become worrisome or controlling.

1. What were some of your worries or fears that tormented you at the time of your abortion?

2. At the time of your abortion, did you ever feel you were losing control, or needed to get in control? If so, explain:

   God's love does not involve torment, because He is never out of control or worried. Knowing the love of God brings a quiet rest.

There is no fear in love; but perfect love casts out fear, because fear involves torment. But he who fears has not been made perfect in love. 1 John 4:18

3. What do you think it means to 'be made perfect in love'?

4. Perhaps your view of God did not include a strong sense of His love at the time of your abortion. Maybe you were counting on the love of others, and they failed you. Their love was not strong enough to give you what you needed. What was the thing you most needed?

5. Looking back at the circumstances of your pregnancy, do you remember a time when you asked God to fulfill your unmet needs?

   At the time of my abortion, I did not put my hope and trust in God's ability to meet my needs. It did not occur to me that such empowering love was available to me. I felt unloved because I had never experienced His love.

   If you have felt unloved, I pray for a greater revelation of His love for you today. Begin to experience His Love by asking Him to reveal Himself to you in the following scriptures.

6. Write what He shows you beside each scripture reference.

   Psalm 48:9-11

   Isaiah 54:10

   John 3:16-17

   I found numerous references to unfailing love in the Bible. All of them referred to *God's* love. You may want to highlight the words, 'unfailing love' in these Psalms. Memorize them by first reading a verse out loud. Then look up and say the verse again. Please spend some time mediating on these Psalms and speak them into your spirit so that they can go from your head to your heart.

Psalm 6:4 - Turn, O Lord, and deliver me; save me because of your unfailing love.

Psalm 13:5 - But I trust in your unfailing love; my heart rejoices in your salvation.

Psalm 31:16 - Let your face shine on your servant; save me in your unfailing love.

Psalm 32:10 - Many are the woes of the wicked, but the Lord's unfailing love surrounds the man who trusts in him.

Psalm 33:5 - The Lord loves righteousness and justice; the earth is full of his unfailing love.

Psalm 33:18 - But the eyes of the Lord are on those who fear him, on those whose hope is in his unfailing love,

Psalm 33:22 - May your unfailing love rest upon us, O Lord, even as we put our hope in you.

Psalm 36:7 - How priceless is your unfailing love. Therefore the children of men put their trust under the shadow of Your wings.

Psalm 44:26 - Rise up and help us; redeem us because of your unfailing love.

Psalm 48:9 - Within your temple, O God, we meditate on your unfailing love.

Psalm 51:1 - Have mercy on me, O God, according to your unfailing love; according to your great compassion blot out my transgressions.

Psalm 52:8 - But I am like an olive tree flourishing in the house of God; I trust in God's unfailing love for ever and ever.

Psalm 85:7 - Show us your unfailing love, O Lord, and grant us your salvation.

Psalm 90:14 - Satisfy us in the morning with your unfailing love, that we may sing for joy and be glad all our days.

Psalm 107:8 - Let them give thanks to the Lord for his unfailing love and his wonderful deeds for men,

Psalm 107:21 - Oh, that men would give thanks to the Lord for His goodness, And for His wonderful works to the children of men!

My Journal

Abba Father — Day 2

Our ancestry is traced through the blood line of our fathers. If you trace back far enough, you get to the first father, Adam. In the beginning was God. Adam was the son of God. God is the father of us all.

1. Read Acts 17:26-28 to find out the relationship that all human beings have with God, the Creator. This passage says that we are His ______.

Now because you are sons, God has sent forth into our hearts the Spirit of His Son, the Spirit who cries out, "Abba!" (That is, "Dear Father!") Galatians 4:6 CJB

The Hebrew word "Abba" is an endearing way to call upon God as Father. In the Hebrew language, every letter of the alphabet has a meaning. The meanings of the letters are combined to give the meaning of the word. The "A" is an 'aleph', and it means the strength or the leader. The 'b' is the 'bet' and it means the house. The term 'Abba' is especially endearing because it means that the leader of the family is in the house giving it strength.

In John 14:23, Jesus says that He and the Father will make their home with us. No matter how abandoned you may have felt in your abortion experience, or anytime in your life, today I pray that you will know that your Daddy is at home.

2. When you were growing up, did you feel secure when your father was home? ___ Yes ___ No Take the time to think about it, and write out how you felt about your Dad being home when you were a child.

   God has given us fathers to model His character. Especially as women, we tend to relate to God in ways that we related to our earthly fathers. The primary role of a father is as a protector of his offspring, bringing provision to the household. If you had a father filling this role model, you felt safe when Daddy was home.

3. At the time of your abortion, what was your father's role?

4. At the time of your abortion, what was your relationship like with your earthly father?

5. How did your father's involvement, or lack of involvement, affect your abortion decision?

6. Please read Psalm 84:11. At the time of your abortion decision, what did you need to know about your heavenly father?

   Genesis 37-47 is the story of Joseph, a man who overcame great circumstances to keep God's perspective. He never let the bitterness of past losses hinder his future. He even managed to keep a positive attitude when his home boys from prison forgot about him when they got out. I believe his success was founded on two concepts in his belief system:

   ◊ He knew the love of the father

   ◊ He developed intimacy with God.

   If we have known a father's love, receiving the love of God may come easier to us. Genesis 37:3 says that Joseph's father loved him more than all his children. He lavished his favor on him. The record of Joseph's life shows that he developed an intimacy with God. Joseph considered himself God's loyal friend. When God gave Joseph a dream, the interpretation was exceedingly favorable to him. I believe Joseph interpreted his dream through his knowledge of God's love. Even in the worst of circumstances, Joseph did the right thing because he was assured of God's love. His heavenly father's love had been modeled by his father Israel, and his concept of God was love.

   Some of us never knew our fathers. We may have grown up feeling that God was distant and impersonal. Some fathers were around, and visible, yet unattached emotionally. They felt distant to us as children. If that was how your father was, you are likely to feel emotionally detached from God as well. Accepting the Creator as your heavenly father may be more difficult if you have broken relationships with your earthy father.

   Yet consider David, who was not so highly esteemed by his earthly father as Joseph. When Samuel came to anoint a king among the sons of Jesse, David was considered so insignificant, that he almost got left out of the picking. Yet David still developed an intimacy with God that made him able to conquer the giant Philistine. He went on to overcome the rejection and insurmountable opposition of King Saul to become King of Israel. David knew the love of the Father. He learned it first-hand from his heavenly Father.

   Some of us had fathers who were themselves in need of healing and regeneration. If your father was not there for you for any reason, such as divorce, death, incarceration, or some type of addiction, you may have a hard time believing that there is a Heavenly Father who cares. Some fathers have unknowingly distorted the picture of God that they were chosen to model.

   But thank God, we have another picture of God's character! We have His Word. When we study His Word, we will discover how our heavenly father relates to us, and find out how to relate to Him.

7. Record what each of these scriptures say about God's relationship to us.

   Psalm 54:4

   Deuteronomy 31:6

   Deuteronomy 33:27

8. Psalm 89:20-26 records what God said about His son David. Please read and meditate on these verses. What were the promises of the One who said that David would know him as his father?

9. No one knew God's heart more than David. Long before he was King, he was learning of God's character. Read what he knew about God in 2 Samuel 22: 2- 20. Write some of the words that David used to describe his personal knowledge of God, his father.

10. The father is also generally seen as the chief provider. If you had a father who filled this role when you were a child, you trusted that you would have your needs met. You probably loved your Daddy, and you may have wanted to be like him. You learned to trust him and expect to be loved. What provision did you need most at the time of your abortion?

11. What did you need to know about God's provision? Complete this sentence:

    If I had understood God's promise of ______________________ at the time of my abortion, I would have made a different choice for my baby.

    Perhaps there are still things you'd like to understand about God. You want more than head knowledge; you want a real experience. Use the journal pages at the end of this day to write these things down. Begin to pray for them. Share them with your group in the next session.

    As adults, we must come to realize that no matter how the picture of God was distorted by our earthly fathers, we are not left with just a picture. We have the real thing! We always have had Him, and we still do. We have a heavenly father who loves us and is there for us. He has been waiting for you to come to Him with trust in your heart.

    When a Father keeps His promises, children grow up trusting Dad's word. God keeps His promises for all His children. A father sometimes makes promises that he isn't able to keep. Some unforeseeable thing gets in the way, or perhaps he simply changes His mind. God is never blindsided about the circumstances, and He is never powerless against them. The integrity of His word is to be trusted.

Our Father God longs for us to come to Him with all our needs. He wants to meet our needs for love and acceptance. He wants to meet all those needs that parents, because of their fallible nature, are able unable to meet. He promises to be a father to us and to never change His mind.

12. What does it take to know God as Father?

    1 John 2:23

    Galatians 3:26

    Psalm 68: 56

13. Who can be called “children of God”? John 1:12-13

    Are you included in any of the above verses? If so, which ones?

    How are we able to call Him “Father”? Romans 8: 12-17

My Journal

A Parent like God **Day 3**

Genesis 1:27 states that God made both man and woman in His own image. God has both male and female characteristics. God is addressed as our heavenly father, but in many ways He is both a mother and a father. God is a tender nurturer, but He is also strong and mighty.

1. Read the following verses. After each verse, decide whether God is being described as a mother or as a father and explain the characteristics you see described.

   Deuteronomy 1:31

   Isaiah 49: 15

   Mathew 7:11

   Luke 13:34

2. What does Isaiah 66:13 reveal about God as a parent?

3. What are some of the ways a mother comforts a child?

   Can you imagine God comforting you in this way?
   Why or why not?

4. What are some of the ways a father comforts a child?

   Can you imagine God comforting you in this way?
   Why or why not?

5. What are three specific ways God comforts us in Zephaniah 3:17?

6. How have you received comfort or support from your parents?

7. Have you experienced God's comfort or support? If yes, please explain.

8. What was your relationship with your mother like as a child?

   What was it like at the time of the abortion?

   What did you need from her that you can now receive from God?

Parents represent the first authority figure of their children. God is the ultimate authority. The way our parents disciplined us as children helps to shape our perception of God's discipline,

9. Write what you see about God's discipline in Revelation 3:19-21.

The parent/child relationship has a natural imbalance of power and authority. How our parents handled that power imbalance shapes how we respond to God. If they used their power and authority to hurt and abuse, we respond to God with fear and distrust.

God's discipline brings correction of the heart. Understanding God's discipline will also help us to train our children the right way. We will train them to respond to goodness with a happy heart. As they grow older, they will likely respond to God's correction in their lives in more productive ways.

10. Read Hebrews 12:5-11. Describe the difference between the way God disciplines us and the way our earthly father disciplines us.

11. A sin or an iniquity is defined by Webster as a gross injustice. According to Psalm 39:11a, why does God discipline His children?

12. Check all the boxes that apply to how you view your abortion experience:

- ☐ It was a mistake
- ☐ An uneducated decision
- ☐ Something out of my control
- ☐ It was a gross injustice
- ☐ Something else. Please explain.

13. Read Hebrews 12:15- 11, especially verse 6, to see who God disciplines.

14. What is God's motivation when He disciplines us? (v10)

15. How do we benefit from God's discipline? (v 10-11)

16. Read Romans 3: 4-5. Does God ever discipline unfairly?

17. Read Romans 2:5-9. What happens if you reject God's discipline?

    One definition of repentance is to *change one's mind*. Repentance is going back to the point where we got off path, and making a different choice. Repentance involves sorrow or regret, but these are the emotions that result from the consequences. True repentance means that we go back to the point of decision and *change our mind*. The way we were thinking then was impure or lacking. God is calling us to a different way of thinking.

18. Read Romans 2:4. What is leading you to go back and change your mind?

19. Read 2 Corinthians 7: 9-10. What is the difference between sorrow over sin and sorrow over the consequences?

20. The parable in Luke 15: 11-31 typifies God's response to those who acknowledge that they have been rebellious and desire to return to their heavenly father. Are there any ways you can identify with the son in this parable? If so, how?

    What is God's response? (v 20)

21. Psalm 39 is a picture of someone suffering from the consequences of their sin. Read Psalm 39 in its entirety. Take this space to tell God your personal feelings about His discipline to you.

My Journal

Husband — Day 4

Webster's defines a husband as a householder. He is a manager or steward of the house. He protects the assets of the house. Proverbs 18:22 says that the man who finds a wife finds a good thing. The role of a husband is to protect his wife as the most valued asset of his life. He protects her physically, as well as emotionally.

1. What does 1 Peter 3:7 say is the role of a husband?

2. At the time of your abortion, what did you want your baby's father to understand?

3. A husband's role is to protect the honor and reputation of his wife by showing her respect. If you were not married at the time of your abortion, there may have been some confusion of the role your baby's father was to play. What does Isaiah 61:7 say that God will give to you?

4. Please read Isaiah 54:4-6: Who is your husband?

5. Verses 5 and 8 reveal another name for God, your husband. What is it?

6. Read Genesis 2:24. In a marriage relationship, the man and the woman are _______flesh. In our covenant relationship with Jesus, we are married to Him.

7. From the beginning, humans were made to be in union with the Creator. When Jesus came, it was God in the flesh, come to reunite God with His creation. He was born in the flesh so that we could be reborn in the spirit. You may be feeling very separate from Him right now, but if you are born again, 1 Corinthians 6:15 - 17 says that you are one spirit with Jesus.

   Think about that! What is the possibility of someone who is one spirit with you being spiritually separated from you?

8. Below are some other scriptures where God is talking about His incredible love for His Bride. Please read these and write a response to God's intimate love for you.

   Isaiah 61:10

   Isaiah 62:5

   Revelation 21:2

   Revelation 22:17

9. Perhaps you never knew the kind of value that God placed on you when He decided that His relationship to you would be as a husband. Perhaps you have been running from Him for a long time, and seeking other lovers. The prophet Jeremiah spoke God's heart to those who were trying to find a satisfying relationship somewhere else besides in God. Please read Jeremiah 3:14. What is God saying to you through this verse?

10. The book of Hosea is a beautiful picture of the love of a husband for an unfaithful wife. Read Hosea 14;4. Even though we may have been unfaithful to God in the past, how does He love us now?

11. No matter how past relationships have distorted your view, God is still there to be a husband to you, if you will let Him. Paul writes in Ephesians 5:23-32 that he is speaking concerning Christ and the church. He describes the role a husband is to play in order to provide a true picture of God as our husband.

    Please read it and write what is most meaningful to you about this passage.

12. What does Ephesians 1:23 say is the church?

13. What does Ephesians 5:30 say that we are?

Exercise:

If you have been in abusive relationships, you may have difficulty believing that God is there to protect, honor, and cover you as a husband. If you feel your mother or your father parented in such a way that you received a distorted image of God, it doesn't have to stay that way. You can now replace these images with the image of the perfect father--your heavenly father. If there was something you lacked from your mother, God can still supply all of your needs. If your husband or significant other did not value you, we can run to a God who will.

Often we unknowingly transfer our assumptions about men or authority figures that we have had in our lives to God. We must consciously recognize that it was not God who behaved in unloving ways, and that His character is different from that of the role models we have been given. Think of the ways that you have been treated by those who should have protected and nurtured you, and write them in the sentences below. Do this as many times as you need to, even if you have to write some in your journal pages.

Complete these sentences:

I am learning to believe that it was not God who

____

I am learning to believe that it was not God who

____

I am learning to believe that it was not God who

____

I am learning to believe that it was not God who

____

I am learning to believe that it was not God who

____

I am learning to believe that it was not God who

____

We can also recognize the good role models that God has given us to show His character. Thanksgiving for these people in our lives will cause us to remember them favorably. Dwell on the good instead of the bad. Good thoughts create an atmosphere for us to dwell with God. Fill in the blanks below with facts about some of the important people in your life.

Dear God, thank you for placing ______________ in my life, who modeled the godly qualities of ____

Dear God, thank you for placing ______________ in my life, who modeled the godly qualities of ____

Dear God, thank you for placing ______________ in my life, who modeled the godly qualities of ____

Dear God, thank you for placing ______________ in my life, who modeled the godly qualities of ____

Dear God, thank you for placing ______________ in my life, who modeled the godly qualities of ____

Dear God, thank you for placing ______________ in my life, who modeled the godly qualities of ____

Dear God, thank you for placing ______________ in my life, who modeled the godly qualities of ____

My Journal

Jesus, my brother and friend — Day 5

The role of a brother or older sibling is to protect and uphold the honor of his sisters. If you had brothers who were distracted with other things, you may not have seen this modeled. Some brothers even exchanged their roles as protectors to that of a predator. This can further distort your view of God as someone you can trust. Precious Sister, you must come to separate what you believe about other male figures from what you believe about God.

1. Read 2 Samuel 13:1-22 This is a story of two brothers of Tamar.

   Who was the bad brother and why?

   Who was the good brother; and why?

2. Who does Romans 8:29 say that Jesus is?

3. Read Colossians 1:15. Who is Jesus a big brother to?

4. How does Jesus prove His love for us? John 15:13

   If you felt abandoned as a child, you may have felt that you were all alone with no one to understand what you needed or how you felt. You needed a close friend that you could trust.

5. Read John 15:12-14 How do you become Jesus' friend?

6. The story of Hagar is recorded in Genesis 16:1- 16. She was a woman abused, mistreated, and misunderstood. Read verses 4-6 and record what happened in each of the verses.

   V 4

   V 5

   V 6

7. Hagar came to know God through the injustice that she endured. How did she acknowledge God's true character in verse 13?

In verse 11 the Angel of the Lord gave her the name for her son, Ishamel. This name is derived from two Hebrew words: "Sh'ma", which means to hear and respond, and "el" which is a name for God. The very name of her son was an acknowledgement that God has responded to her crisis pregnancy by responding to her cries in the wilderness.

8. At the time of your abortion did you think God could see your or hear you?

9. What was your impression of God's seeing you? What were some of the things God would have heard and seen then?

10. The fact that God sees and hears everything can be comforting, as it was with Hagar, or it can be unsettling. There may be things in your life that you would rather God did not see. In what ways are you comforted by the fact that God saw and heard you?

11. Proverbs 24:11- 12 says, "Deliver those drawn toward death, and hold back those stumbling to the slaughter. If you say, 'Surely we did not know this,' Does not He who weights the hearts consider it? He who keeps your soul, does He not know it?" God even sees our heart. He knows our fears and our intentions. Is there anything in your abortion experience that you have been trying to hide from God? You can share your heart with Him honestly now by writing your prayer of confession in your journal.

This Week In Review

Review this lesson on God's relationship with us and complete the following statements in your own words.

My relationship with God before the study was…

____

I can now think of Jesus as my best friend because…

____

My heavenly father is …

____

God is my husband because…

____

My Journal

Discovering the Roots

Session 3

See, I have this day set you over the nations and over the kingdoms, to root out and to pull down, To destroy and to throw down, To build and to plant. Jeremiah 1:10

A lie is like a seed; if left underground it will sprout and take root. When we believe a lie, we cultivate it. When we act on the lie, it produces fruit. The fruit of a lie is death.

Abortion is death. When an abortion has taken place, the fruit proves that there were already implanted lies. Those lies often remain there to justify the abortion. The goal of this session is to discover the lies that are rooted in the abortion decision, so that they can no longer produce death. You and I want the beliefs that caused us to make such a grievous decision to be pulled up by the roots, so that we will be able to rebuild our lives as a fruitful garden, giving glory and praise to our Creator.

Choose who to listen to **Day 1**

1. John 8:44 are the words of the Son of God. He makes mention of a spiritual force of evil in this verse. Jesus calls him 'the devil', and says that he speaks a lie. Since you cannot see the devil, how do you think the devil can "speak a lie?"

   What are the devil's' desires?

2. At the time of your abortion, what was your heart's desire?

3. Was there a time when you thought about whether abortion was right or wrong?

   Do you think that God was trying to speak to you then?

   Why do you think you were not able to "hear" Him?

   I can hear the broken heart of Jesus in John 8, verse 45 saying, "because I tell the truth, you do not believe Me". Exploring the history of our decision-making will help us to see the points where we were listening to the wrong voice. In every situation of our lives, God has been there. Bad choices and the consequences that follow come from listening to the wrong voice. If we listen long enough, we begin to believe. We eventually act on what we believe.

   Everything that you presently believe is rooted in a first time experience. Fact is, nobody decides to have an abortion unless they have first learned to believe a lie somewhere. These lies could be false beliefs about you, or about God. Unless you are willing to go deeper into your belief system than the abortion decision, you will likely not root out the lie. As long as it is still there, it can still produce death. This time what gets aborted may be a relationship, an opportunity, or your God-given destiny.

   We can make a choice now to listen for the voice of God. Under no circumstances would I ever want you to revisit an event just to feel condemned or to re-experience a temptation or trauma. What we will do in our session is slow down the negative experiences in our lives enough to see what we really have believed. Starting right now, we are going to practice listening for the voice of God and hearing the truth. When we do this, we actually reframe our past, by responding to the truth instead of a lie.

   Every emotionally traumatic event in your life has a strong belief attached to it, whether good or bad. Journeying through some of the highs and lows of your memory banks can help you take a closer look at your belief system.

4. If you are willing, jot down the first five or six things you remember that were emotionally significant in your life.

   Then, use the Lifeline on the next page to chart your emotional history. Rate emotionally significant positive events above the center horizontal line, with a 10 being pure joy. Rate emotionally significant negative events below the center line, with a 10 being absolute devastation. Keep the events in chronological order, beginning with early childhood at the far left, proceeding to current adulthood at the far right. The purpose is to uncover the significant life hurts and help you understand patterns of behavior in your life.

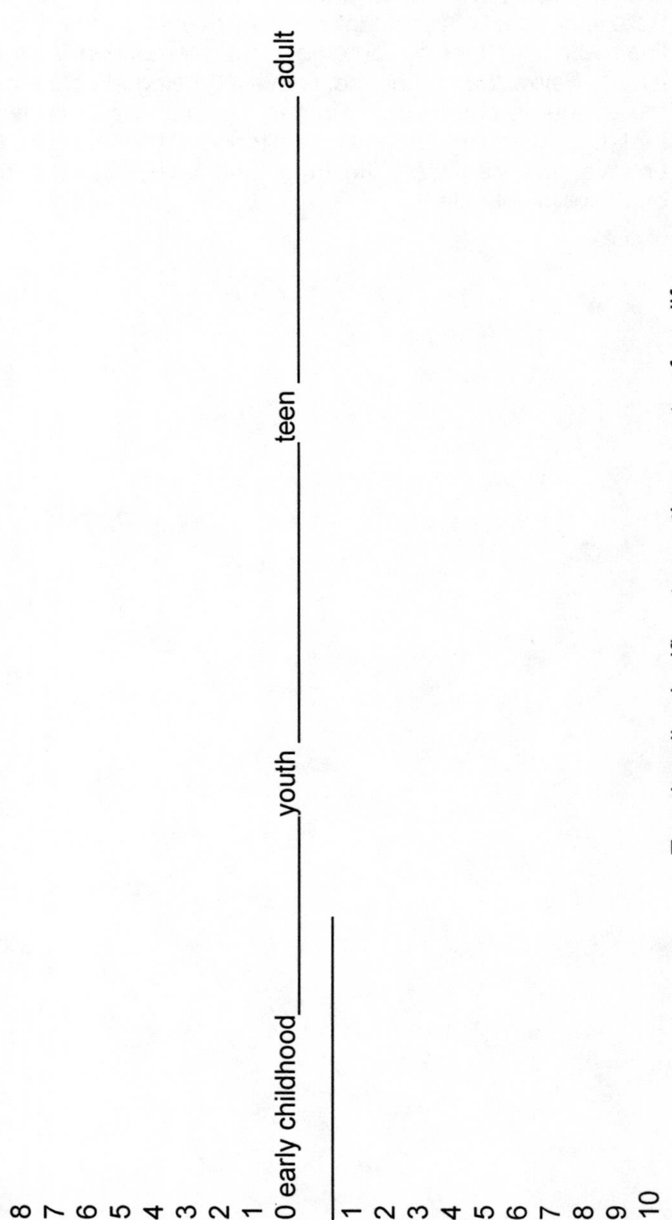
LIFELINE
Emotionally significant positive events in my life
10
9
8
7
6
5
4
3
2
1
0 early childhood
youth
teen
adult
1
2
3
4
5
6
7
8
9
10
Emotionally significant negative events of my life

Choose to break the curse **Day 2**

A curse is a misfortune or torment that comes in response to an action. Curses mean we are off track from God's intended purposes. They keep us from walking in the blessings of God and fulfilling our purpose for which we were created. The torment may be emotional and spiritual. The misfortunes that follow can affect our health, our finances, and our circumstances. Ultimately, they prevent us from reaching our intended destiny.

1. God is talking to Abraham in Genesis 12:1-3. He is speaking to him about his intended destiny. What does God intend for Abraham?

   What will happen to those who curse Abraham?

   Who will do the cursing?

   God's' intended purpose for Abraham was to bring forth a nation from his family. It was a covenant promise. The original covenant is sometimes referred to as "the Law". It is meant as a tutor to show us the seriousness of obeying God's instructions. When we violate the commandments of God, we bring ourselves out of line with His intended blessing. When He set the universe in order, He established moral law. We can choose whether to obey it or not; but we cannot choose which consequences come with our choice.

   God is the judge of the universe. He judges individuals and entire nations as a remedy to our waywardness. Curses can actually be disciplinary measures that will bring us back into alignment with God's' will. The ultimate will of God is that we be blessed.

   Some people think of curses as being projected onto them as witchcraft. While we will certainly consider the power of the spoken word, let's get things into perspective.

2. Let's' go back to God's original plan in Genesis 1:28. After God created man, what was the first thing He did for them? He _____________ them. Most precious child of God, this is still His intention for you. Let's' work with Him on it!

   Read the rest of Genesis 1:28. Fill in the blanks to show the other things God did for mankind.

   He gave them a command to be _______________ and multiply; to fill the earth and ____________ it; and to have _______________ over everything in the sea, the air, and on the earth. The command was a condition to the blessing. How does abortion break the condition of this blessing?

3. Read these definitions of the key words in this passage. Then, return to Genesis 1:28 and meditate on the first thing that God said to mankind.

sub due [sub ***b***-*doo,* —verb

A. to conquer and bring into subjection

B. to overpower by superior force; overcome

C. to bring under mental or emotional control; as by persuasion or intimidation; render submissive

D. to bring under cultivation

do·min·ion [duh-*min*-**yuh** ***n]*** –noun

A. the power or right of governing and controlling; sovereign authority

B. rule; control; domination

C. a territory, usually of considerable size, in which a single rulership holds sway

D. land or domains subject to sovereignty or control

E. government

We have been empowered with blessings and authority in the earth. God's' intention for us did not change because of our misbehavior. Read Proverbs 26:2. If a curse without a cause cannot alight; then we would do well to look at causes for repeated patterns of torment or misfortune in our lives, and eradicate them.

Evil spirits are only given access to us through passive consent and active choices that we make. The curse that results is a consequence that brings us back to a full knowledge of our separation from God. In our pain and loss, we will cry out to Him and come back to Him. That is His ultimate desire.

Can you think of some patterns of behavior in your life that you would like to get rid of? What are they? What about repeated misfortune? Is there a pattern of accidents, losses or poverty? What about patterns of mental torment or repeated negative emotion?

4. List whatever comes to mind in the following table:

behavioral patterns	mental / emotional patterns	patterns of misfortune

The New Covenant does not erase the lessons of the original covenant. Jesus ushered in the New Covenant with grace and truth, and ratified it with His Blood. We now have the power and authority to break a curse in our life, no matter how it got there.

An Old Covenant prophet who spoke before the period of silence was Malachi. He spoke of the last Old Covenant prophet, John the Baptist. Yes, we read about John the Baptist in the New Testament, but remember, he was before the New Covenant was ratified by Jesus' Blood. John the Baptist was the spirit of Elijah that Malachi prophesied of. The curse was broken through Jesus.

Remember the Law of Moses, My servant, which I commanded him in Horeb for all Israel, with the statutes and judgments. 5 Behold, I will send you Elijah the prophet before the coming of the great and dreadful day of the Lord. 6 and he will turn The hearts of the fathers to the children, and the hearts of the children to their fathers, Lest I come and strike the earth with a curse. Malachi 4:4

5. To understand generational curses, Read Exodus 20:5-6

Write a summary of what you just read here:

This commandment establishes the fact that one generation affects another spiritually. At the time of this writing, people lived longer, and it was possible for the 3rd and 4th generation to live around the aged head of the family. This means his or her behavior would have an effect on the next generation as they grow up and learn what behaviors are acceptable. Generational curses are picked up from the sins and patterns of behavior of our parents or leaders that have gone before us.

The spirit of abortion was given legal ground when the highest courts of our land made a judicial decision to sanction abortion legally. Its effects are being felt in this generation.

Sometimes curses are passed on to us spiritually through unconfessed sin of the ancestors. For instance, the Biblical patriarch Abraham had a habit of practicing deception. He lied about Sarah being his wife on two occasions. He raised a son, Isaac, who did the same thing regarding his wife, Rebecca. Then Isaac's son, Jacob, deceived him in order to receive the inheritance of his brother Esau.

What has been passed down to you from your family? Have you come from a family with a long line of alcoholism, drug addiction, poverty, abortion, or incarceration? If a curse has been operating generationally, you may feel greater affects from it than you are responsible for. Feeling the effects of the sins of our family and shouldering the guilt of others are two different repercussions. God brings healing to the former and relieves the unnecessary burden from the latter. He actually gives you the power through faith in the shed blood of Jesus to break the curse of the former generations, and establish a blessing for you and your offspring to a thousand generations! Wow! What a Good God!

You cannot shoot an enemy that you cannot see, especially if you don't even know it exists. Below is a list of Biblical Curses. Recognize where patterns in your family blood line are taking you outside God's' blessings.

- Check the ones that you feel might apply to you.
- Then read the accompanying scriptures.
- Pray to break the curses by using the steps to freedom on page 35.

Possible Causes of Curses

- ☐ Willingly deceiving others Joshua 9:22-23
- ☐ Adultery Job 24:15- 18
- ☐ Fornication Deut 22:22-24
- ☐ Disobedience to the Lord Deuteronomy 11:26- 28
- ☐ Murder Genesis 4:10-11
- ☐ Pride Psalms 119:21
- ☐ Intercourse with family member Deuteronomy 27:20- 23
- ☐ Homosexuality Leviticus 20:13, Romans 1:27
- ☐ Sodomy Deuteronomy 27:21, Leviticus 20:15-16
- ☐ Raping someone Deuteronomy 22:25_27
- ☐ Dishonoring Father or Mother Deuteronomy 27:16
- ☐ Cursing or striking one's parents Exodus 21:15_17
- ☐ Causing the unborn to die Exodus 21:22_23
- ☐ Attempting to turn someone away from the Lord Deuteronomy 13:5-9
- ☐ Doing anything that is punishable by death Deuteronomy 21: 22-23
- ☐ Idolatry Jeremiah 44:8
- ☐ Children born out of wedlock Deuteronomy 23:2
- ☐ Being a thief Zechariah 5:4
- ☐ Breaking a vow to God Zechariah 5:4
- ☐ Taking money to kill the innocent Deuteronomy 27:25
- ☐ Not staying a virgin until married Deuteronomy 22: 13-21
- ☐ Human sacrifices Leviticus 20:2
- ☐ Being a rebellious child Deuteronomy 21:18-21
- ☐ Being tattooed Leviticus 19:28

Choose Freedom

1. Confess and acknowledge your sin or the sin of your family members. Ask God for forgiveness, and forgive the family members.

2. Using the power of the spoken word, command the curse to be broken ex." In the name of Jesus Christ, and by the authority that He bought through His blood, I break this curse of ______________________.

3. Command all demon spirits associated with the curse to leave you immediately in the name of Jesus. You can do this quietly. The power is within you, not in how loudly you say it.

4. Ask God for His Kingdom nature to replace the void.

My Journal

Choose what side you're on — Day 3

1. Read chapter 18 of Ezekiel. In the space below, write a summary of God's' attitude in this passage.

   What evidence of God's mercy do you see in this chapter (verse 23)?

   Do you detect a pleading coming from the heart of God at any point in this chapter? If so, what was He pleading for people to do? (V 21, 24, 26)

   Finally, look at Ezekiel 18, verses 14 and 31. In very simplified terms, how is the chain of destructive behavior broken?

2. Read Deuteronomy 30:1-20. Do we have a choice in whether to be cursed or blessed by God? (Verse 19)

   List some of the blessings that come with the choice of life mentioned in this passage.

   What is the curse of God in verse 18?

   How difficult is the choice? (Verses 11–14)

   Our actions are direct results of the way we think. Mental curses keep us from thinking the thoughts that line up with God's plan for our lives. Wrong thinking produces wrong choices. Wrong choices bring a curse upon our lives. When these negative patterns of misfortune or misbehavior continue in our lives, we are said to be 'under a curse'.

   Would you like to train your mind to think right thoughts? You can do it with a little practice! The first step is discerning what thoughts are from God and what are not. When you experience a negative emotion, stop and ask yourself, "Is this God?" If it's' not, you can then choose whether to accept or reject the thought. When you reject it, replace it with God's' perspective.

The Words Of God And The Words Of Satan.

The Holy Spirit Gives:	Satan Gives:
1. Sense of holiness	1. Sense of worthlessness
2. God consciousness through the Word	2. Self-consciousness through feelings
3. Clarity	3. Confusion
4. One task to do at a time	4. Clamoring: pressure to do everything now
5. Correction	5. Accusations
6. Voice of conviction	6. Voice of condemnation
7. Conviction of unconfessed sin	7. Condemnation of past sins already dealt with
8. Encouragement to obey (hope)	8. Discouragement leading to despair (loss of hope)
9. Confirming peace	9. Frustration and pressure
10. Balanced Life	10. Bondage

3. Read 1 Peter 5:8 What does the apostle Peter call the devil in this passage?

   Some curses are a direct satanic attack. An enemy or adversary is not someone you play games with. If you allow these thoughts, you will eventually come into agreement with them. You cannot defeat an enemy that you have agreed with.

4. At the time of your abortion decision, you probably heard many voices. List some of the thoughts you had when you were trying to make the decision about what to do about your pregnancy. Also remember how you felt about those thoughts. *What were your feelings?* Then, check where you now think those thoughts were coming from.

I thought about____

Looking back, I think that was probably from _____ God or _____ My Enemy

I thought about____

Looking back, I think that was probably from _____ God or _____ My Enemy

I thought about____

Looking back, I think that was probably from _____ God or _____ My Enemy

What about your present thought life? Start to think about what you are thinking about on a daily basis. Journal some of your thoughts. Which side of the chart on the previous page do most of your thoughts line up with?

My Journal

Spiritual Warfare **Day 4**

1. Ephesians 6:12 speaks of spiritual warfare. Name the four kinds of demonic forces that war against our souls.

   1. ____________________ 3. ____________________

   2. ____________________ 4. ____________________

   A principality is a territorial prince over other accompanying spirits. The powers spoken of here are spiritual, unseen forces. They gain territory when we start to believe the lies that are coming from the murderer, the enemy, our adversary the devil.

2. Ephesians 1:15- 23 is a prayer for spiritual wisdom. After reading this passage, write down who has authority over the spiritual principalities and powers. In Luke 10:19, Jesus delegated His authority to His disciples. If you are a disciple of His, then this authority belongs to you. Authority always comes the responsibility to exercise it properly.

3. Read Mark 16:17 What signs did Jesus say would follow those who believe in Him?

   A strongman is a spiritual power that has been given strength by human agreement. Mark 3 teaches that If we try to bind strongmen, and then have fellowship with accompanying spirits, we will remain a house divided.

4. Please read Mark3: 23—27 before going on.

   The chart on the next page shows some of the strongman spirits that operate in an abortion decision. Remember the feelings and the thoughts you had when you were trying to make a decision about your pregnancy. Ask the eternal Spirit to show you what spirit was operating, and what agreements you made. Wherever you make an agreement with a lying spirit, that spirit begins to govern your thoughts and actions. Some of what I was feeling was....

   Some of my thoughts were.....

If you see some of the accompanying spirits operating in your life today, it is time to bind the strongman. Perhaps they became a part of your belief system before the abortion. Perhaps they have been plaguing you since then. Either way, it is time to be vigilant against your adversary, and give these thoughts no more rights to your mind.

Strongman	Accompanying spirits	Kingdom nature
Pride	Stubbornness, gossip, controlling spirit, arrogance, self-righteousness, religious spirit, covetousness, greed, contentions, wrath, anger, mockery, scorn, egotistic, haughty, vanity, judging	Humility
Idolatry	Unfaithfulness, whoredom, homosexuality, fornication, prostitution, adultery, love of the world, love of money, love of food, all sexual sins, abortion, emotional weaknesses, unequal yokes, unclean, and foul spirits	Faithfulness
Lying	Superstition, divination, witchcraft, hypocrisy, strong delusion, exaggeration, vain imagination, criticizes man of God, perversion, homosexuality, profanity, false visions, insinuation, driving spirits, vain notions, deception, lust, condemnation	Truth
Murder	Jealousy, rage, anger, abortion, suspicion competition, revenge, restlessness, cruelty, hate, selfishness, division.	Love

5. Are you being affected by any of the spirits listed? If so, ask God when this started. Confess the sin, ask forgiveness from God, renounce the sin, and turn from it. Then you have the authority in Christ to bind the strongman spirit and command all the accompanying spirits to leave you.

   No curse without a cause can alight. When we give these spirits no place, they have no cause to operate in our lives. Ask the Lord to fill you with His Spirit to replace the void. The column on the right lists the nature of God that will fill the void left by a strongman spirit that you have renounced. Maybe you feel so cursed that you do not have the power to do this now. Read 2 Peter 1:3 to see whose power you must rely on for everything that is needed in this moment. When in small group session, ask your leaders to pray with you.

My Journal

Power of the spoken word — Day 5

Unfortunately, other human beings are used of Satan to speak curses over our lives. In Genesis 1 God "spoke" the world into existence. Later he made man "in His image". The words we speak have power because we are made in the image of God,

1. Read Proverbs 18:21. What kind of power does the tongue have?

2. Read James 3: 1-10 to see the power of the spoken word.

According to verse 9 we bless God, but ______________________ man. Has someone ever told you that you were stupid, worthless or that you would never amount to anything? Perhaps someone told you that you had ruined your life because of the pregnancy. Those are spoken curses over your life. These words have power and if spoken often enough, cause you to believe them. What you believe is what you act out. Lies can be as powerful as the truth if you come into agreement with them.

Today you have a choice to believe what the word of God says about a believer in Christ and start turning those beliefs around. Use the "Created in the Image of God" brochure to be transformed by renewing of your mind in His Word.

My Journal

War on the Seed

Session 4

And I will put enmity between you and the woman, and between your seed and her Seed; He shall bruise your head, and you shall bruise His heel. Genesis 3:15

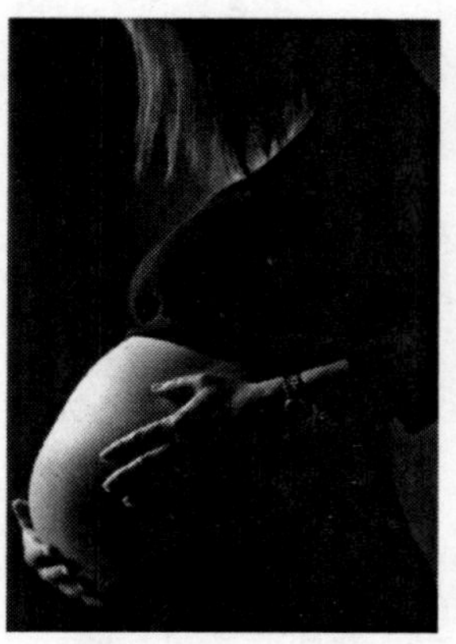

The time of pregnancy can be very confusing. The God-given desire of a mother to give life struggles with the less-than-perfect circumstances.

In the best of circumstances, a woman may feel loved and honored during her pregnancy. She wants to nurture her baby's life. It's a part of the very purpose for which she was created. Pregnancy is a time in a woman's life when she gets to participate with God in the miracle of new life!

We begin bonding with our baby at the moment of conception. Our souls become linked to a new human being. We are motivated by pure love. There is a desire to see our child become all that he will be. We'd like to help him develop his talents and gifts. We wonder if he will be like mommy or like daddy. We want to help plan all the birthday parties, graduations, weddings, and other celebrations of life. We want to share our experiences of life, and help him make choices. We want to share in his wonder as he discovers his world. We want to participate in God's unfolding plan for his life.

Motherhood is an honorable profession. It is a high calling and an opportunity to have a long-term effect on the world. Yet many mothers in crisis pregnancies find their position challenged and their role dishonored. A mother with child who has been abandoned can be vulnerable physically and emotionally. She's become responsible for a new human being, and she needs security more than ever. Everything revolves around the pregnancy and she feels a sense of urgency to do something about it. If the child was conceived in a non-committed relationship, she is especially vulnerable. The support that she should have a right to is just not there. The adverse circumstances of the pregnancy seem to overshadow the God-given desire to nurture life. There is a daily torment over the decision. There is war on the seed.

As we grope with the reality of the pregnancy, we are moved by what we see. We can see the circumstances with our natural eyes. We are vaguely aware of the baby, but we cannot see him or her. The known circumstances are perceived as more real than the baby who is unseen. The spiritual forces of darkness are in the unseen realm, warring against the seed.

As the baby grows, our bond with him grows stronger. We become increasingly aware of the humanity of the fetus. The confusion about what to do builds up an anxiety. Anxiety turns to fear; fear to panic. The pressure is on for a solution. Do we choose to have the baby, or end the pregnancy? We tell ourselves the problems will go away if we just end the pregnancy. The challenges of our situation become the fears that minister to us on a daily basis. The more we meditate on the fears, the more real they seem. One day, we wake up, fear overshadows us, and we get an abortion.

Coming out of the abortion clinic, we enter into a **relief phase** because the daily torment is finally over. We're no longer struggling to make a decision; it's already been made. The length of the relief period varies greatly among women, depending on the way they process grief, what other things are going on in their lives, and their spiritual state at the time of the abortion. Relief is a stage of processing a loss. Denying the loss is a way that we respond to sin. We don't want to think about the loss. If we did, we would have to face that fact that what we have lost is indeed our own child.

Eventually, the same mental and emotional struggle that was present at the time of the pregnancy starts to resurface. We start to question our decision, and rethink our options. We start to employ coping strategies to keep from having to face the loss. Coping strategies are psychological mechanisms that we use to defend our position. We might revisit the memories of the situation, and justify our choice based on our circumstances. We rationalize that it was the "best choice", and we deny that anyone else was affected by that choice.

Still, we feel sad, shameful, and guilty. We *feel* guilty because we are guilty. God has set the boundaries of blessing within what is right by His standards. God's boundaries don't change because of our circumstances. Rather, circumstances change because of the boundaries that we choose.

Create in me a clean heart, O God , And renew a steadfast spirit within me, Do not cast me away from Your presence, And do not take Your Holy Spirit from me. Psalm 51: 10-11

When the old lies start to resurface, we cannot seem to convince ourselves that everything is alright. We feel distanced from God and we long to get back. No matter how much we analyze and rethink our decision, we still feel pain. People will tell us we are forgiven, or that it was a wise choice and best for everyone, but we still feel something is very wrong. Our need for healing goes beyond being pardoned; we need the pure heart that will bring us back into fellowship with our Creator.

When does life begin? — Day 1

Does life begin at conception, at birth, or sometime in the womb? The Creator's answer to this question was written long before the technology was developed to so that we could see with our natural eyes. The writings of God's prophets recorded that which was confirmed by science millenniums later. We can trust the authority of the written word of God.

1. How far along in your pregnancy were you when you had your abortion?

2. What did you personally believe about when life begins at the time of your abortion?

3. What do the following verses reveal about God's view of when life begins?

   Genesis 1:26-28

   Job 33:4

   Isaiah 46:3

4. When did your unborn baby's life begin?

5. Read Romans 1: 18-19. Can you remember a time when your conscience tried to tell you of the wrongness of abortion? How did you respond?

6. If you would like, you can ask your facilitator to share a booklet about fetal development. Trace your unborn baby's physical development until the time of the abortion. Record three facts that impress you about life in the womb.

7. Does God have a specific plan for every life? Acts 17:26-28

8. Read these verses and write who is being spoken of, and what God's specific plan is for each person.

   Jeremiah 1:4-5

   Psalm 139: 13-16

   Luke 1:15

   Luke 1:31

9. How did you find out about the option of abortion?

10. What were your thoughts about the legality of abortion?

11. Read Proverbs 14:12 Are the laws of man the same as the laws of God?

My Journal

The Decision — Day 2

1. How did you find out you were pregnant? How did you respond?

2. What were your thoughts and feelings when you first became aware that you might be pregnant?

3. In Genesis 3:4 what lie did the serpent tell Eve about the consequences of eating the fruit?

   What did you believe about the consequences of abortion?

4. In Genesis 3:5 what lie did the serpent tell Eve about God?

   What did you believe about God's part in your decision to have an abortion?

   - ☐ He doesn't know (He doesn't see me)
   - ☐ He doesn't care (He won't intervene)
   - ☐ He understands that this is the only thing I can do.
   - ☐ I didn't really think about Him.

5. In Genesis 3:6 Eve saw three things before she ate the fruit. What were they?

   What benefit did you believe that abortion would bring you?

6. Read 1 John 2: 16 to understand what is NOT of God. Please fill in the blanks.
   Lust of the ____________ (wanting to gratify ourselves)
   Lust of the ______________(being tempted by what we can see)
   ____________ of Life (being concerned about what people think)

7. Which of the three things in 1 John 2:16 most enticed you to choose abortion?

8. The last line in Genesis 3:6 says that Eve also gave to her husband with her, and he ate. Was there anyone in your abortion experience that you convinced to agree with you about the abortion?

9. Genesis 3: 13 records Eve's confession of wrong. Who does she say deceived her?
   Was there anyone who deceived you in your abortion experience?

10. Whom did you tell when you knew you were pregnant?
    Record the reactions that each person expressed and advice they gave.

11. Did you feel pressure from the opinions of others that influenced your decision to abort?

12. Whom did you choose not to tell and for what reasons?

13. Did you receive counseling? What was the advice you received?

14. Who besides yourself did you allow to have the major influence on your decision?

15. Did you feel rushed to make your decision? For what reasons?

16. What resources or information did you need to make a good decision? Were these things available to you?

17. Who took the responsibility for the final decision on abortion?

18. Was there someone you were seeking to please at the time of your abortion? Read Galatians 1:10 and write your response here.

19. Are there any areas about the decision that you can't recall?

20. Accepting the fact that abortion ended a life is the first step in grieving. Facing this truth allows a woman to understand that her emotional response to her abortion is the response to losing a child.

    Complete the following statements.

    I had an abortion to relieve the pressure of ...

    I had an abortion because I felt anxious about...

    I had an abortion because I was afraid others around me would think...

    One thing I told myself in order to deny the loss was...

    The point at which I could no longer deny my loss was...

    One thing I understand now that I didn't know then is...

Created to nurture — Day 3

Our Creator gave women the natural instinct to nurture and protect their babies.

1. 1 Kings 3:16-28 records Solomon's first public display of the wisdom God gave him. Solomon was offered anything he wanted from God. He chose wisdom to govern his people. After reading the passage, write which woman had the true heart of a mother.

   While you are not still the same woman today that you were at the time of your abortion, which of these women would you have identified with at the time?

2. Did you want your baby?
   Why or why not?

   What about today?
   If you feel differently today, what changed your mind?

3. What were the Hebrew women ordered to do with their sons in Exodus 1:22?

   In what ways was the situation of these mothers similar to your own?

4. What did Moses' mother do? Exodus 2:1–3

5. What was your opinion of abortion before your pregnancy?

   - ☐ I considered myself pro-life
   - ☐ I considered myself pro-choice
   - ☐ I was neutral on the subject

6. Read 1 John 2:15–16 again, please. What kind of love hinders our love of God?

When we have an abortion, the pain of facing the truth is so great, that we become very good at putting up our defenses. We hold tightly to the lies we clung to at the time of the abortion, keeping our feelings at a distance. Many of us have managed to put it out of mind through some very carefully laid defenses. Some have been so busy medicating their pain that they have forgotten what hurts.

Some of the same things we believed at the time of the abortion are continuing to 'clone' themselves in other situations. They've become a part of our belief system, yet we refuse to look closely at them because we don't want to feel the emotions that are connected to the beliefs. As long as the lies are still there, they will continue to do damage to our relationship with God and others. We find ourselves unable to obey the truth.

Since you have purified your souls in obeying the truth through the Spirit in sincere love of the brethren, love one another fervently with a pure heart, having been born again, not of corruptible seed but incorruptible, through the word of God which lives and abides forever. I Peter 1:22-23

In order to purify our hearts and reform the belief system that led us to choose death, we must follow those feelings to understand what we actually learned to believe. We must revisit the abortion experience and allow the Holy Spirit to show us the truth, and the Living Word to replace the lies.

When we shut down our emotions, we shut down both good and bad emotions. We will never have the passion for God we desire without revisiting some painful places and allowing Holy Spirit to heal them.

Remember the war is against the Seed. The abortion was only one battle. We are still in the war. If you are born again, then an incorruptible Seed of God's Son lives on the inside of you. That Seed is what brings about your God-given purpose in life. Your healing is creating a fertile place for that Seed to take root. Lies are bad seed. When you allow yourself to feel again, you are weeding out the lies that try to choke your inheritance from God.

My Journal

Your sexuality — Day 4

This course is about rooting out thoughts and behaviors that steal from us. The sexual act was the beginning of the pregnancy. It is important to look at the conception as part of the abortion experience because this was when the responsibility for the abortion began. The timing and circumstances of the pregnancy were a choice. The consequences of that choice led to another choice—------the abortion.

1. How did you meet the father of the baby?

2. When did you first decide to engage in sexual activity in this relationship? Did you take the active or passive role in this decision?

3. What external pressures led to that decision?

4. What internal pressures led to that decision?

5. What was your understanding of the relationship?

6. What did you tell yourself about the possibility of becoming pregnant at that time?

7. Did you discuss the possibility of pregnancy with the father of the baby? What was his understanding?

   What was yours?

8. What were your beliefs regarding sex before marriage?

9. If you knew God's will, would you want to do it?
   If so, read 1 Thessalonians 4:3 and record what it says here.

10. Please read 1 Peter 2: 11–12. What does this verse say about the war?

11. How do you think the soul is involved in a sexual act?

    Sexual intercourse is a covenant. In a covenant, the two are made as one. You take on a piece of the soul of your sexual partner, and he or she takes on yours. Every time you have a sexual partner, you leave a piece of your soul with them. Your soul is made up of your mind, your will, and your emotions. Every part of your soul has the ability to commune with another person's soul.

    One woman wrote, "I had so many partners; I was spread out all over the place. My mind was distracted, my will was only to get more drugs to forget who I had become, and I was emotionally numb. I felt separated from God. Wholeness was not even a concept I could grasp. I felt fragmented. I felt the real me was lost somewhere along the way."

    Psalm 88 describes this condition. Pieces of this person's soul have been trapped in spiritual places – in the grave, and in the pits. Verse 8 speaks of the bondage of sexual sin:, " I was "shut up, and I could not get out".

12. We are going to study 1 Corinthians, Chapter 6 to learn more about God's instruction for sexual blessings. First read verses 1517. What do you think it means to be "joined" to someone in soul and spirit?

    If we are joined to someone spiritually, we become one with them. In a sense, we are also joined to other partners that they have had. This manifests in our soul and in our body. Just as sexually transmitted diseases can be passed from one partner to another, our spiritual union is a point of transmission of spirits.

13. Please read verses 19 and 20 again. Why are we being warned to "flee sexual immorality"?

14. Can sexual immorality rob you of your inheritance in the Kingdom of God? Read verses 9 and 10 for the answer.

15. See Galatians 5:19 and Ephesians 5:3. Webster's defines fornication as consensual sex between two persons not married to each other. What does the One who created us say about this?

16. What is our body made for? (1 Cor 6:13)

17. If we use our bodies in a way that is not intended by our Creator, what can happen? (Rom 1: 26–27

My Journal

The power for purity **Day 5**

For this is the will of God, your sanctification: that you should abstain from sexual immorality; that each of you should know how to possess his own vessel in sanctification and honor, not in passion of lust, like the Gentiles who do not know God; that no one should take advantage of and defraud his brother in this matter, because the Lord is the avenger of all such, as we also forewarned you and testified. For God did not call us to uncleanness, but in holiness. Therefore he who rejects this does not reject man, but God, who has also given us His Holy Spirit.
1 Thessalonians 4:3-8

One of the things that women who have had abortions often say is that they'd like to be close to God again. They are seeking the intimacy that the union with their partner promised to produce, but failed them. They feel unclean, taken for granted, and dishonored. Intimacy with God brings a sense of honor and security, knowing that all is right. You can remove the stains of sexual sin through faith in His word today and achieve the intimacy with God that you have desired.

1. Read 1 Corinthians 6:12 to see how sex can bring us under its power.

2. What does 1 Peter 1:5 say will keep us?

3. According to 2 Peter 1:3, what does His power give us?

   Sometimes, intimacy with God is lost through the shame of sexual promiscuity. I remember hoping that God didn't see. When you regain your sexual purity, it will bring you to a new level of intimacy with God. Do you want to break the soul ties of the past and be a pure bride of Christ? Following are some steps to freedom from ties to past sexual partners. It may take some time, but God can purify you. The steps are coupled with sample prayers and scriptures to meditate upon.

Breaking ties with sexual partners

1. **Ask the Lord to reveal to you every occasion where you used your body sexually as an instrument of unrighteousness.**
   Holy Spirit, You are the Spirit of Remembrance and of Truth (John 14:26; 15:26) Search me and show me where I have given my own body over to the bondage of being one with other human beings and the spirits that have ruled them. Show me where I have opened a door to evil spirits that are holding me captive to do Satan's will.

2. **Renounce previous or current sexual involvements**
Father, I renounce the unrighteous use of my body. I have dishonored you and my own body in the passion of lust. I have shunned your love by ignoring your boundaries. (1 Thess4: 3-6)

3. **Acknowledge the truth that God's instructions on sexual behavior are the right standard.**
I thank You that in Christ my sins are forgiven, but I have transgressed Your holy instruction and given the enemy an opportunity tot wage war in my members (James 4:1; 1 Peter 5:8)

4. **Ask God to forgive you for each specific unrighteous use of your body.**
I acknowledge that I have used my body as members of unrighteousness and allowed an open door to sin to have dominion over me. I ask for not only pardon, but also purity. (Romans 6:12-13; I John 1: 9)

5. **Forgive others for their involvement with you, whether it was forced or consensual, so that you will not hinder your own freedom.**
Lord Jesus, You said if I forgive men's sins, they shall be forgiven. (John 20:23) Your blood was shed for the remission of sins. I remit my ties to individuals with whom I have participated in my idolatry and rebellion against you. I ask for my freedom from them, and for their freedom from bondage to me. (1 Thess 4:3-6)

6. **Annul each covenant made through sexual union outside of your present marriage.**
By the Blood of Jesus, the blood of the new covenant that was shed for me, I break my covenant ties with _________ *and all spirits bound to him(her). Their effects are annulled and no longer have dominion over me. (Is 28:18, Rom 6: 9-14)*

7. **Humble yourself before God regarding your weaknesses in this area.**
Holy Spirit of God, I need your help. I have allowed myself to go beyond what I knew that I could withstand and refused to look for the way out of temptation that You provided. In my weaknesses You are made strong, as I rely on Your power over sin. I have made provision for my flesh. Help me to set the boundaries so that I will not bring myself into temptation. Help me to hear Your voice and to love You with all my heart, all my mind, and all my strength. (James 1:21; Rom 13:14; 2 Cor 12:9)

8. **Ask God to fill you with the Spirit and renew your mind daily.**
Lord of all Creation, my body was created by you for your glory. I accept the payment of Jesus' sacrifice for my life. I want to glorify You with my life as a new creation. I now ask You to fill me with Your Holy Spirit. I submit my body to You as an instrument of righteousness, a living sacrifice, that I may glorify You in my body. I commit myself to the renewing of my mind in order to prove that Your will is good, perfect and acceptable for me. (Rom 12:2, Titus 3:5; 1 Cor 6: 20)

My Journal

Who's Responsible?

Session 5

You will keep him in perfect peace, whose mind is stayed on You, because he trusts in You. Isaiah 26:3.

Feelings of anger are a normal part of any loss, and it is normal for a woman who has experienced an abortion to be angry. Traumatic losses produce great pain. There's the sense of "I hurt, and someone's going to pay." The pain of the loss forces the issue of responsibility. The woman's anger may be directed at those she loved and trusted the most during the time of her decision. She may be angry with God for not stopping it, or with herself for being blinded, fearful, or not strong enough. There may be a sense of betrayal because of the reactions of others and self-doubt because she didn't expect to feel this way. These issues all stand in the way of grieving the real loss: the baby.

Anger is a very powerful emotion. It is one of the strongest of human passions. When anger arises, it demands a response. Anger does not go away on its own. Denied, it finds ways to express itself and tends to form roots of bitterness.

Anger is a God-given emotion that indicates something is very wrong. It needs to find a way of expression. Anger expressed without self-control is destructive, hurting many who stand in its way. An angry life may become characterized by sarcasm, hostility or vengeance.

How I learned anger — Day 1

Our life experiences from childhood and beyond have taught us ways of reacting to the emotion of anger. People deal with (or fail to deal with) anger in different ways, depending on our history and our personality. As we grow, we watch our parents and learn to imitate the ways they express their anger. Later in life a spouse or significant other may express anger in unhealthy ways, and we develop ways of responding to them. Understanding how and what we have learned helps us evaluate the need for change.

Answer the following questions to discover what you have learned from others.

1. How did your father express his anger? What did he usually say or do when he was angry?

2. How did your mother express her anger? What did she usually say or do when she was angry?

3. How did your spouse or significant other express his anger? What did he say or do when he was angry?

4. What was it like for you to be around each of these people when they were angry? What do you feel?

5. How do you express your anger? What do you do and say?

6. Which of the above people are you most like when you express your anger?

7. What is it like for others to be around you when you express your anger? Are you willing to ask those who live with you for their input?

8. In what ways would you like to express your anger differently? Write this as a prayer in your journal today.

9. Memorizing and meditating on the following proverbs can help you. Begin by looking them up and writing them out.

   Proverbs 15: 1 ____

   Proverbs 29:11 ____

   Proverbs 29:22 ____

10. According to Galatians 5:22-25 how can you have self-control?

11. What does self-control lead to?

    James 1:19-20

    2 Peter 1:5-8

12. What are the ways you can choose to control your anger?

13. Self-control is something that takes practice. Think of a time when you became angry this past week. What was your response? If you had used self-control in this situation, what would have happened? What would have been prevented?

My Journal

What does anger look like in me? Day 2

Anger does not always look like a fit of wrath. Some personalities tend to push the anger down. Eventually it will find a way to express itself. Suppressing and denying anger is no healthier than exploding in rage. Anger suppressed can take the form of sarcasm, cynicism, depression, or lack of motivation. The following is an evaluation tool to help you discover if you are experiencing anger. Everyone will recognize some of these characteristics. The goal of the evaluation is to help you identify areas that you would like God to change in you. Check the statements that apply to you.

- ☐ Impatience comes over me more frequently than I would like.
- ☐ I nurture critical thoughts quite easily.
- ☐ When I am displeased with someone, I sometimes shut down communication or withdraw.
- ☐ I feel inwardly annoyed when family and friends do not comprehend my needs.
- ☐ Tension mounts within me as I tackle a demanding task.
- ☐ I feel frustrated when I see someone else having fewer struggles than I do.
- ☐ When facing an important event, I may obsessively ponder how I must manage it.
- ☐ Sometimes I walk in another direction to avoid seeing someone I do not like.
- ☐ When discussing a controversial topic, my tone of voice is likely to become passionate and strong.
- ☐ I can accept a person who admits his or her mistakes, but I have a hard time accepting someone who refuses to admit his or her own weaknesses.
- ☐ When I talk about my irritations, I don't really want to hear an opposite point of view.
- ☐ It's hard for me to forget when someone does me wrong.

- ☐ When someone confronts me from a misinformed position, I am thinking of my rebuttal as he or she speaks.
- ☐ Sometimes my discouragement makes me want to quit.
- ☐ I can be quite aggressive in my business pursuits or even when playing a game just for fun.
- ☐ Although I know it may not be right, I sometimes blame others for my problems.
- ☐ When someone openly speaks ill of me, my natural response is to think of how I can defend myself.
- ☐ Sometimes I speak slanderously about a person, not caring how it may harm his or her reputation.
- ☐ I may act kindly on the outside while feeling frustrated on the inside.
- ☐ Sarcasm is a trait I use in expressing humor.
- ☐ When someone is clearly annoyed with me, I too easily jump into the conflict.
- ☐ At times, I struggle with moods of depression or discouragement.
- ☐ I have been known to take an "I don't care" attitude toward the needs of others.
- ☐ When I am in authority role, I sometimes speak too sternly or insensitively.

If you are experiencing ten or more of these traits in your life, anger is to some degree controlling your life. It will rob you of the blessings of God, and of relationships that He has intended for you to have. But don't give up! The first step in resolving the anger is identifying it. Unresolved anger causes a frustrating cycle.

The painful circumstances of your abortion may have caused you to feel devalued, that your worth as a person was being insulted. Maybe you didn't know who or how to ask for what you needed. Maybe your needs were unmet or ignored. Maybe someone showed disregard or contempt for your values, convictions, or your motherhood. That painful circumstance caused an angry emotion. Later in life, when similar situations occur, your response could be heightened simply because the historical event was never resolved.

sAsk God to show you where it began. He will take you back to the place where the cycle of anger started.

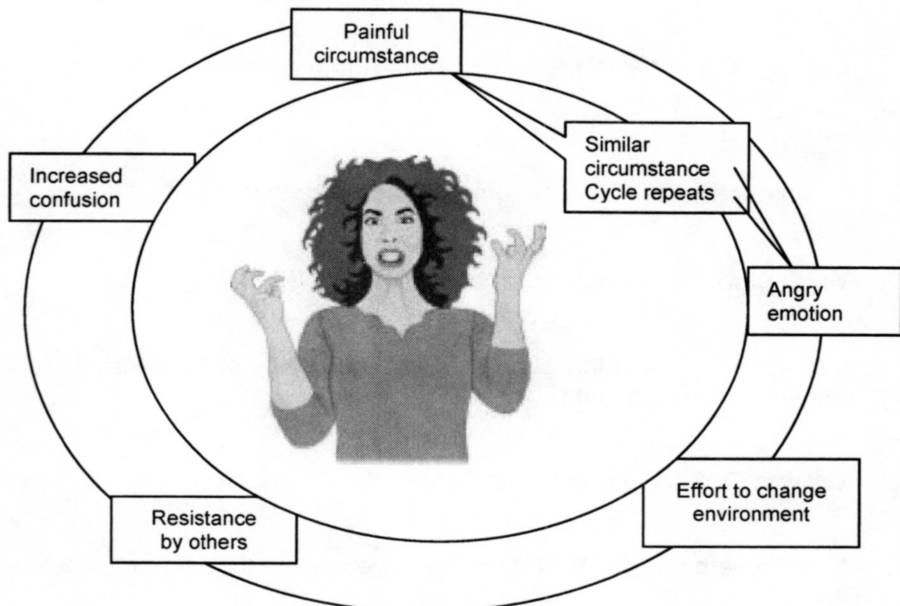

You must face the angry emotions of your abortion honestly. Facing your anger head-on can be painful, because you have to think about the hurtful circumstance again. When you feel the anger, think of what it was that you needed. What did you believe that you were without? Beloved, whatever it was; it does not have to be so. Jesus is our all in all. He really will answer all our prayers. He will come and satisfy our every need in due time. When we place our trust in Him, we do not have to be angry or frustrated. He brings peace even in times of lack, and assures us that everything is going to be OK, as long as we keep walking with Him. Let's walk with Him through His word.

Anger demands a response. We can choose to respond to God or to the circumstances. It's not the anger that causes so much trouble; it's the reaction after the emotion. Let's first look at God's anger to see how we should respond when we are angry. We who are made in His image shall become like Him. What drives His anger? What results from His anger?

1. How is God's anger described in the following verses?

   Psalm 78:49

   Deuteronomy 29:28

   Psalm 90:7

2. What characteristics of God influence His anger?

   Exodus 34:6–7

   Psalm 33:5

   Psalm 78:38

3. For what reason is God slow to anger according to Isaiah 48:9?

4. Why God was angry with Solomon in 1 Kings 11:9-10?

5. Read verses 5 – 8 of this chapter. What were some of the behaviors that revealed Solomon's heart?

6. Why was God angry with the Israelites in Deuteronomy 9:7?

7. Read Proverbs 6: 16-19. Record the seven things that are detestable to God.

8. Do you think God is angry with you for acts similar to those described in the previous questions? If so, which ones?

9. Should you be afraid of God's anger (Ps. 90:4–11)?

10. How did the psalmist experience God's anger in Psalm 76:7?

11. How was the psalmist able to have hope in the face of God's anger (Ps. 130:3–4)?

12. How can we be saved from God's anger and experience his forgiveness?

    Acts 13:38

    Romans 5: 8–11

    1 Thessalonians 1:9–10

What motivates my anger? Day 3

Anger in and of itself is an emotion, not a sin. The emotion is a natural part of grieving a loss. There is a proper response to anger. Our motivation will determine the way in which we respond. Will we react to the circumstances, or will we respond to the empowering love of God?

Today we'll look at some ways that Jesus responded. Ask Holy Spirit to show you His heart as you search the scriptures.

1. Read Mark 3:1-6. Why did Jesus feel angry (v.5)?

2. Was His response productive?

3. Did Jesus ever sin when He was angry?
   (Hebrews 4:14–15)

4. Carefully read John 2:13–16.
   List the causes of Jesus' anger.

5. Did Jesus react, or did He premeditate His response? (v15a)

6. What changes took place for the better because of His response?

7. What time of year was it? (v 13)

8. What did the Jewish people sacrifice at this time of year?

9. What was Jesus called in John 1: 29?

10. What was Jesus' purpose in coming to the earth? 1 John 3:5

11. In 1 Peter 1:18-19 what is Jesus compared to?

    God gave the sacrificial system to His people Israel as a forerunner of His ultimate plan of redemption. The sacrifices that were taking place in John 2 represented the sacrifice that Jesus would make as the Lamb of God who came to take away the sins of the world. It was a picture of the redemptive nature of God. But many were distorting the picture through buying and selling instead of giving and sacrificing.

    On the last week that Jesus lived, he repeated this same scene in Luke 19: 41-46. Many people call this "The Passion Week". Jesus' grief for what sin had done to the lives of the people was at its highest level. He came to redeem us from the affects of sin. His passion for our loss that made Him angry.

12. What does Luke 19: 41 reveal about what Jesus was feeling?

13. What did He do about it? (verse 45)

14. Read Ephesians. 4:26.

    Is anger a sin?

    What is it we are NOT to do concerning anger?

15. Why do you think God instructs us not to be angry for more than a day?

16. What is it about our nature that explains why we need this guidance in expressing our anger (Rom 1:29-32; Rom 7:18; Gal 5:19-21)?

17. Give examples from your own life when the expression of your anger came from your sinful nature.

18. What was it you needed from the person who made you angry?

19. How can you now trust God for the things that you need?

My Journal

Hurting people hurt people — Day 4

When people are hurt, their first response is usually anger. The expression of anger may be an attempt to hurt others as they were hurt. If people believe that the actions of others against them were not right in God's eyes, they may feel justified in getting even.

1. What does the Bible say about wanting to get even?

   Proverbs 24:17-18

   Romans 12:19

   2 Thessalonians 1:6

2. Is there anyone in your abortion experience that you would like to see hurt as much as you hurt? If so, how have you responded to this anger?

3. What are some of the ways God wants you to respond?

   Romans 12:20-21

   Ephesians 4:32

   Colossians 3:13-14

4. In what ways can you respond to your post-abortion anger, according to the above verses?

   Abortion is an experience that leaves many women feeling angry. If your experience was recent, your anger may be fresh. If your abortion was years ago, this anger may have formed roots of bitterness in your life. Women often remain angry with those they loved and trusted the most during their experience.

5. What are you to do with your old anger?

   Ephesians 4:31

   Colossians 3:8

6. What happens if you do not get rid of this anger?

   Ephesians 4:26–27

   Hebrews 12:15

   1 John 2:9–11

7. Do you have any areas of anger that you have tried to cover up or hide? Has God been speaking to you about any areas of post-abortion anger?

   Even a little thing can sometimes cause a root of bitterness. Let's get passionate about rooting out anger. To help determine who or what may be a root of resentment in your abortion experience, do this exercise with me.

   First, make a list of everyone who was involved in your abortion experience. It's not about figuring it out; it's about your *feelings*. This includes the pre-abortion decision, and the actual act. It could even include people that did not know anything about the pregnancy, if they played a part in your decision. Who do you *feel* is responsible in any way? Make an honest list here.

Now assign a portion of this pie to the people you *feel* are responsible, with the most responsible having the largest portion.

Looking back at the pie, assign a fraction or a percentage to each of the portions.

Eradicating roots of bitterness **Day 5**

1. How do we get out of the darkness of anger?

   Ephesians 5:11

   1 John 1: 6-7

2. Read Hebrews 12: 14–17. Write your response to God in this space.

   Bitterness in your heart cannot be hidden or denied. It must be addressed. God commands you to get rid of it. One of the ways you can get rid of it is to bring it out of the darkness and into the light.

   Quiet your heart and ask God to show you any areas of bitterness left from your experience. Ask him to show you any person with whom you may still be angry. Put that person before your face and remember what they did to you. Write a letter to them as though God were standing right there in the room as you spoke to them. Beloved, God is standing right there. You may want to use some or all of the phrases below to help you express your true feelings. Write down the specific ways this person has hurt you. Do this for everyone who got a portion of your pie. This exercise is only meant to bring what has been in the darkness for so long out into the light, so God can heal it.

THE LETTER IS NOT MEANT TO BE SENT.

I am angry with ____________________for ________________________________

It hurt me when ____.

At times, I have been confused about what you did to me. On the one hand,

I felt, ______________________ on the other hand I felt ___________________.

I get mad every time I remember how you ____________________________.

I resented it when you ____

I used to get angry when you ____

I felt __________________________ when you ___________________________

It makes me feel sad to remember how you ____________________________

Now I sometimes have trouble trusting because __________________________

I wish that____

Something I want that may be more realistic is __________________________

Oil of Joy Instead of Mourning

I am angry with ____________________ for ________________________________

It hurt me when ____.

At times, I have been confused about what you did to me. On the one hand, I felt, ______________________ on the other hand I felt __________________.

I get mad every time I remember how you ____________________________.

I resented it when you ____

I used to get angry when you ______________________________________

I felt __________________________ when you __________________________

It makes me feel sad to remember how you ____________________________

Now I sometimes have trouble trusting because _________________________

I wish that ____

Something I want that may be more realistic is ________________________

I am angry with ____________________ for ________________________________

It hurt me when ____.

At times, I have been confused about what you did to me. On the one hand, I felt, ______________________ on the other hand I felt __________________.

I get mad every time I remember how you ____________________________.

I resented it when you ____

I used to get angry when you ______________________________________

I felt __________________________ when you __________________________

It makes me feel sad to remember how you ____________________________

Now I sometimes have trouble trusting because _________________________

I wish that ____

Something I want that may be more realistic is ______________________

I am angry with __________________ for ___________________________

It hurt me when ____.

At times, I have been confused about what you did to me. On the one hand, I felt, ____________________ on the other hand I felt _________________

I get mad every time I remember how you ___________________________

I resented it when you ____

I used to get angry when you ______________________________________

I felt ________________________ when you _________________________

It makes me feel sad to remember how you __________________________

Now I sometimes have trouble trusting because _______________________

I wish that ____

Something I want that may be more realistic is ______________________

I am angry with __________________ for ___________________________

It hurt me when ____.

At times, I have been confused about what you did to me. On the one hand, I felt, ____________________ on the other hand I felt _________________.

I get mad every time I remember how you __________________________.

I resented it when you ____

I used to get angry when you ______________________________________

I felt ________________________ when you _________________________

It makes me feel sad to remember how you __________________________

Now I sometimes have trouble trusting because _______________________

I wish that ____

Something I want that may be more realistic is ____________________

The next step in getting rid of this bitterness is to forgive people who have hurt you. Forgiveness is not easy, especially when hurt may have been with you for years. You have taken an important step this week in getting honest with God and others. Next week we need to look at the reasons why we are angry with ourselves. Then we will be ready to apply God's plan for forgiveness. Come to class ready to share honestly about your hurts.

I am angry with ________________for ________________________

It hurt me when ______________________________________

At times, I have been confused about what you did to me. On the one hand,

I felt, ________________ on the other hand I felt ______________

I get mad every time I remember how you ______________________

I resented it when you ________________________________

I used to get angry when you ___________________________

I felt ____________________ when you __________________

It makes me feel sad to remember how you ____________________

Now I sometimes have trouble trusting because __________________

I wish that ____

Something I want that may be more realistic is ____________________

The next step in getting rid of this ____________________________

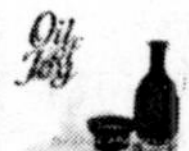

Guilty Feelings

Session 6

Deliver me from blood guiltiness, O God,
The God of my salvation, and my tongue shall sing aloud of Your righteousness. Psalm 51:14

Last week, we discovered that anger has to find a way to express itself. When the emotion arises, remember that God is there. God has a way of allowing us opportunities to practice what we are learning from Him. Ask Him to show you why the emotion is surfacing, and what it is that you really believe about the situation you are in. Look for new ways to respond to the provision of God. His love will empower you!

Personal Responsibility — Day 1

When we have lost something, the sense of personal responsibility leads to guilty feelings. Since the Garden of Eden, man has reacted to his losses by blaming others. When Adam and Eve committed the original sin, they felt ashamed and hid from God. They lost the most precious thing we have in life: fellowship with God. Read Genesis 3:12 to see how Adam reacted.

1. Who did he blame? ________________ and ___________________
2. Who did Eve blame? (v 13) _________________________________

When there seems to be no one else to blame, some women direct their post-abortion anger inward. This brings on a host of other problems. The guilt and anxiety over the wrongness of the decision often entangle women in a web of self-condemnation and self-pity leading to low self esteem. The pain of the loss is entangled with our own guilt. There seems to be no outlet.

We try to find ways to cope with it. It seems too heavy to bear. We try to shift the burden in some way. Drugs and alcohol, eating disorders, sleep disorders, and becoming involved in abusive or dishonoring relationships are all behaviors that indicate we have turned our anger inward. Our own life becomes devalued in our eyes because we've denied the sanctity of our children's lives.

Guilty feelings left unresolved turn to condemnation. Take this self-test to see if any of these feelings or behaviors apply to you.

Condemnation of Self	**Condemnation of Others**
☐ Self debasing statements	☐ Verbal Abuse
☐ Low Self Esteem	☐ Nagging Criticism
☐ Feelings of unworthiness	☐ Fault-finding
☐ Substance Abuse	☐ Physical Abuse
☐ Eating Disorders	☐ Criticizing overweight people
☐ Not Accepting complements of others	☐ Withholding appreciation and/or affection
☐ Neglect of Health or hygiene	☐ Ignoring Friends and Family

Guilt results from breaking one of God's laws. Guilty feelings come as a result of transgressing the moral code that is inherent in all human beings.. When the code has been violated, justice demands payment. God provided that through His Son. If we repent and stop doing what we feel guilty about, our guilt is covered by His plan of salvation. We can accept that covering only by faith. Guilty feelings still linger when we *choose* not to accept God's plan of salvation.

1. Do you still *feel* guilty about your abortion experience? If so, list the reasons for your guilty feelings here. What do you feel guilty about? Ask for forgiveness for any unconfessed sin.

2. In what ways have you tried to cover your guilt?

3. Please read Hebrews 10:17-22

   Does God remember our sins? (v 17)

Is there any payment we can make to cover our guilt? (v 18)

What is the payment Jesus made for sin? (v 19)

Verse 22 says that we may draw near to God with a __________ heart and in full assurance of _____________.

4. Please read Titus 3:4-7. Now read it again and meditate on God's attitude toward sinners revealed in this passage. Try to memorize this passage.

Fear of punishment — Day 2

Often abortion leaves us with a sort of free-floating guilt that can't be named. After all, what we did was legal, and approved by at least some segments of society. In some cultures, it was "just what you did". Why then, do we feel as though the shoe is going to drop? The hammer is going to fall? Why do we feel like the worst could happen at any minute? We wake up anxious, and our days are driven by performance. Some women even feel cursed, as if they could do nothing right.

If we feel guilty fear of punishment can control our relationships. Below is a self-test to help you determine if fear of punishment is operating in your life. Write in the number that best describes how often the following situations occur for you.

1	2	3	4	5	6	7
Always	**Very Often**	**Often**	**Sometimes**	**Seldom**	**Very Seldom**	**Never**

__________ 1. I fear what God might do to me.

__________ 2. After I fail, I worry about God's response.

__________ 3. When I see someone in a difficult situation, I wonder what he or she did to deserve it.

__________ 4. When something goes wrong, I have a tendency to think that God must be punishing me.

__________ 5. I am very hard on myself when I fail.

__________ 6. I find myself wanting to blame people when they fail.

__________ 7. I get angry when someone I think is bad prospers.

__________ 8. I complain about others when I see them doing wrong.

__________ 9. I tend to focus on the faults and failures of others.

__________ 10. God seems harsh or unavailable to me.

__________ Total

If your score is:

57-70 God has apparently given you a very strong appreciation for His love and unconditional acceptance. You seem to be freed from the fear fo punishment that plagues most people. Some people who score this high either are greatly deceived or have become callous to their emotions as a way to suppress pain.

47-56: The fear of punishment controls your responses rarely or only in certain situations. Again, the only major exceptions are those who are not honest with themselves.

37-46: when you experience emotional problems they may relate to a fear of punishment or an inner urge to punish others. Upon reflection, you will probably relate many of your previous decisions to this fear.

27-36: The fear of punishment forms a general backdrop to your life. There are probably few days that you are not affected in some way by this fear. Unfortunately, this robs you of the joy and peace your salvation is meant to bring.

0-26: Experiences of punishment dominate your memory and have probably resulted in a great deal of depression. These problems will remain until some definitive plan is followed. In other words, this condition will not simply disappear; time alone cannot heal your pain. You need to experience deep healing in your self-concept, in your relationship with God, and in your relationships with others.

≥ 50:You will need to take action to overcome these tendencies. Love must be the motivating factor in our decision-making, not fear.

Please read our signature scripture of Isaiah 61:1–3 again. The vengeance of our God is directed on the enemies of our soul, NOT on us. Why did Jesus proclaim this passage in Luke 4? It is because His sacrifice was the provision for us. We can now take the punishment that was due us and turn it on our spiritual enemies. Remember that the Lord proclaimed His favor upon you in Isaiah 61:2? Part of having God's favor means that He has provided vengeance for our enemies. The key word in the NIV version of Isaiah 61:3 is *instead*. Read it in your Bible to see what we get *instead*.

________________________ *instead* of ashes.

________________________ *instead* of mourning

________________________ *instead* of a spirit of despair

Beloved, we can trade our punishment for favor if we learn to apply it in spiritual warfare. God has given you the neck of your enemy. Your feelings are a smoke trail to where the enemy has attacked you. Today we are going to start the Divine exchange by proclaiming the trade, just as Jesus did when He read Isaiah 61 to His homeboys in Nazareth.

First we are going to make a list of the feelings that we experience in regard to past guilt. Be as honest as you can about this, because the truth will set you free. I will start the list to help you out. You can add any feelings that you regularly experience. Then, I want you to write in what you want from God ***instead.***

1.	______________________	*instead of*	☐	Helplessness
2.	______________________	*instead of*	☐	Hopelessness
3.	______________________	*instead of*	☐	Anxiety
4.	______________________	*instead of*	☐	Nervousness
5.	______________________	*instead of*	☐	Failure
6.	______________________	*instead of*	☐	Fear of ______________
7.	______________________	*instead of*	☐	____________________
8.	______________________	*instead of*	☐	____________________
9.	______________________	*instead of*	☐	____________________

Now start asking the Lord for the Divine exchange. Ask the Lord for His promise to you in the area where you need to make the exchange. Ask your small group leader to help you with scripture that you can memorize and pray, and start claiming your inheritance from the Lord. He has highly favored you, and he is not wearing the colors of the enemy.

My Journal

The face of shame — Day 3

Shame is guilt that has been internalized. "I'm guilty" means "I did something wrong", but shame says, "There's something wrong with me." Most women experience shame following an abortion. The abortion procedure is so intensely personal that it is difficult not to internalize the feelings that it generates. Think about how you were treated when you went to have the procedure. How did it make you feel? What part of your abortion experience still makes you feel ashamed? Write your shameful feelings on this frowning face, exposing all the things the enemy is trying to impose upon you.

4. Isaiah 61 promises honor instead of shame. What other promises does God give in His Word about relief from shame? Is there a condition to these promises?

   Psalm 25:3

   Psalm 34: 4–5

   Isaiah 54:4–8

   This is a definition of the word ***scorn.***

   1. *open dislike and disrespect or derision often mixed with indignation*

   2. *an expression of contempt*

   3. *an object of extreme disdain, contempt, or derision: something contemptible verb: to treat with scorn.*

5. In what ways can you scorn the shame of your past?

   2 Corinthians 4:2 2 Timothy 2:15 1 John 2:28

   Another way that the enemy will try to torment us is through fears of the unknown. Anxiety is a type of fear. Anxiety following an abortion may be mild, a sort of nagging in one's mind accompanied by thoughts like, *I wonder if it was a boy or a girl?" or "I wonder if my life would be like this if I had kept my baby?"*

6. Are there questions in regard to your abortion that repeatedly plague your mind? What are they?

7. What will happen if you let these anxieties continually dwell in your heart? Luke 21:34

8. Write what God shows you to do with these anxieties in the following scriptures.

   Psalm 55:22

   1 Peter 5:7

9. What is the one very important way you can relieve your anxieties? (Phil 4:6-7)

10. What helps you when you are anxious?

    Take a few moments now to pray about your anxieties. It may help to write out your prayer here.

    Ask God to show you someone who would be a good prayer partner with you. Write what He shows you here. Then look for an opportunity to pray for her needs, and she will become someone you can pray with.

11. Think back to a time when you felt anguish in your abortion experience. How would you describe your environment then?

    What was our anguish like?

12. What physical changes did Jesus go through as he prayed in anguish? (Luke 22:44) What does it feel like in your body when you are in anguish?

13. What was the answer the psalmist found in his anguish? (Ps 18:6–16)

14. Tears may be a big part of anguish. What does Psalm 6:6 say about weeping in anguish?

15. What promise does God give in Psalm 126:5 regarding tears?

16. What does God do with all your tears? (Ps 56:8)

17. In times of anguish the truth of Romans 8:26 can be a great source of comfort. What is that truth?

My Journal

Depression **Day 4**

Anger, guilt, and shame turned inward results in depression. In Psalm 38 David describes his feelings of guilt.

1. Write in your own words the symptoms of depression found in each verse and circle the ones you have personally experienced.

2. How does David find relief from his guilt? (Ps 32:5–7)

3. Many times depression feels like being in bondage, chained to a sorrowful emotional state. Read Psalm 107:10-11. What were the prisoners feeling and for what reasons?

   Have you felt any of these feelings? Do you know the reasons for your feelings?

   Can you draw a picture of what it feels like to be in bondage?

4. What helped the prisoners in Psalm 107:13–14 in their deepest gloom?

5. From what bondages does God promise to set you free?

   Romans 8:18–22

   Galatians 5:1

   Depression results from our feelings of shame and guilt. Jesus bore those things. We can make a decision to accept that, and become empowered by His love for us. Depression also results from our feelings of sorrow and grief that go unrelieved because of the loss of our children. This type of depression is a necessary step in grieving that loss. There is a piece of our soul attached to them. Yet, there is no place in our society to mourn the loss of an aborted child. God has purposed in His loving heart to give you a safe place to mourn your loss through this study and in the class.

6. Esther 4:1–3 describes the Old Testament ritual of mourning. What were some of the things they did to let others know they were mourning?

7. What were some of the ways you mourned your loss of your baby at the time of your abortion?

8. In Lamentations we find many verses describing Jeremiah's heartache Which of the verses in Lamentations 3:48–51 describe your experience following your abortion?

9. Where did Jeremiah find relief (Lam 3:21–26) ?

10. Describe some of the ways you have found relief from your heartache.

11. What does God promise to those in mourning?

    Psalm 30:11–12

    Isaiah 61:1–3

    Often depression is the direct result of self-focus. The more we are focused inward, the worse we feel and the harder it is for us to take the necessary steps to health. What advice do the following Scriptures give on how to break this cycle?

12. Where should your eyes be focused? Hebrews 12:1–2

13. Where should your mind be focused? Colossians 3:2

14. What is your attitude to be?

    Ephesians 4:22–24

    Philippians 2:5–7

    1 Peter 4:1

15. Which of these verses will you remember when times of depression come? Write it down, memorize it, and meditate upon it daily.

My Journal

Your life is valuable to God — Day 5

When I agreed with abortion, I agreed with death. Subconsciously I felt that if my baby was better off, then I might be better off dead too. My suicide attempt was a desperate attempt to escape the pain of living with abortion. Suicidal thoughts plague many women who regret their decision to abort their unborn baby. Reasons vary but somewhere there is an agreement with death implanted in the belief system of that women. Often she feels unworthy to live after having taken her baby's life. She may want to join her child in heaven. Many women do not want to face future relationships because of their past experiences. Many are angry at society for making them feel so alone in their feelings of regret. Many fear facing God. Beloved, if you have felt like ending your life, facing God is exactly what you need to do. He stands with open arms ready to save.

1. In Numbers 11: 1-15 Moses asks God to let him die. What is the answer God gives in verse 17?

2. Are you letting others help carry your burden of sorrow? Who have you allowed to help carry your burdens? Are you reluctant to share this burden with anyone with whom you are close?

3. According to Psalm 68:19 there is someone who bears your burden for you each day. Who is that?

4. According to the following scriptures, what moral responsibilities do people have toward one another?

   Romans 15:1

   Galatians 6:2

   1 Thessalonians 5:14

5. Judas betrayed Jesus and then committed suicide. (Matt 27:5) Peter also betrayed Jesus by denying him three times. Please read Luke 22:61-62 to see how Peter's response differed from Judas's. .

6. Do you identify more with Moses or Peter?

   Do you believe God will comfort you as he comforted these people?

7. What do these verses say about the life of a person who has returned to relationship with God through His Son?

   2 Corinthians 5:17Galatians 2:20

8. In John 10:10 Satan is compared to a thief. What does he want to do to you?

9. What kind of life did Jesus come to give you?

   John 5:24.

   John 10:10

10. God is the author and sustainer of our lives. To honor God means to love the life that He has made. Use this space to write a prayer to God thanking Him for your life. Honor Him as the only life-giver. If you have entered into relationship with God's Son, you can make the promises in the above scriptures your own.

My Journal

Experiencing Forgiveness

Session 7

But without faith it is impossible to please Him, for he who comes to God must believe that He is, and that He is a rewarder of those who diligently seek Him. Hebrews 11:6

The truth about abortion leaves us with a heightened sensitivity to our need for forgiveness. We are plagued by guilt, shame, and heaviness, and we long to be free of the heavy burden. We have many unanswered questions about God's forgiveness that keep us from coming back to Him. Does God forgive? Does He forgive everyone or only some? Does God forgive someone who had an abortion when she knew it was wrong? Are there degrees of sin? Is a first trimester abortion as bad as a third trimester one? These questions can be answered through His Word and through our experience with Him.

Many people feel that God has forgiven them, yet they still refuse to forgive themselves. What this really means is that they feel their sin is so great that they don't deserve to be forgiven. They must make some kind of offering as proof that they have really changed so that they can feel worthy of forgiveness. Until then, they will simply hold onto their guilt.

The truth is no matter what we do, we have nothing to offer God for the price of our sin. We cannot forgive ourselves. If we could, then we would not need a savior. Paul wrote to the Believers in Corinth, "For I delivered to you first of all … that Christ died for our sins." (1 Cor 15:3) The first step in forgiving yourself is to accept that forgiveness is through Christ's death alone. Recognizing this truth is the beginning of accepting *His* plan of forgiveness, not ours. Isaiah 59:16 says that God provided salvation by *His own arm*. Embrace His plan, and you will go from repentance to refreshing, from guilt to gladness, and from grace to glory.

Your journey from guilt to glory begins with trust in God. Trust His plan. Go after Him with all your heart. Trust in His goodness, His kindness, and His mercy. Trust most of all in His love. He wants you free to live, free to love, and free to fulfill your destiny. It is His great love that is drawing you nearer to Him. He is more intent on reconciling His relationship with you than you are. He will reward any effort you make to come home to Him because He wants you.

Read Hebrews 11:6. What is another word for trust used in this passage? Please memorize this verse using the word “trust”. Begin by writing it right here. Say it to yourself every day as you seek to experience His forgiveness.

A woman after God's heart **Day 1**

David was a man after God's heart. He was destined to be a king, but there was a time in David's life when he felt the weight of sin. Through the fire of deep repentance, his heart was cleansed anew. That is why he could say, "Wash me, and I *shall be* whiter than snow. Make me hear joy and gladness, that the bones You have broken may rejoice." (Psalm 51:7-8) You too are destined to rule in God's kingdom. God is after your heart.

David committed a sexual sin that led to death. As such, he was guilty of murder and at least partially responsible for the death of his own child. He was king, but he was as much in need of God's forgiveness as you or I have ever been. God promised David that his offspring would rule over Israel forever (I Kings 9:5). He did not withdraw His promise because of David's sin, though it was very great.

The first chapter of the gospel of Matthew records David's line leading to Jesus. The fact is, God brought forth from the line of David an eternal ruler, Jesus, who is the King of Kings! In Mark 10: 47_48, a man cried out to King Jesus as he walked the streets of Israel. When he asked Jesus for mercy, he addressed him as "Son of David."

David's story gives us hope that God can restore our joy when we have humbled ourselves before him in deep repentance. I am convinced that the more we see the depravity of our own heart, the greater revelation we have of God's incredible mercy. That is what caused me to fall in love with God. As the Holy Spirit shines His light on the places in your heart that He wants to cleanse, don't be afraid to cry out to Him, "Son of David, have mercy on me!"

Let's start our study with David's prayer of repentance recorded in Psalm 51 to answer the following questions:

1. What two characteristics of God's nature did David recognize in verse 1?

2. Was David conscious of his sin or still in denial? (verse 3)

3. In verse 2, David asked for cleansing from *sin* and from *iniquity*. What do you think is the difference between the two?

4. Can you hear David's quest for the truth evidenced by verse 6? This inner cleansing is what made him a man after God's own heart. He was

not afraid to look at the sin that was "ever before" him. In verse 10 he cries out, "Create in me a clean heart, O God." Perhaps David had seen the wickedness of his heart that led him down the path to death. He needed more than pardon; he needed purity.

My own abortion did not happen as an isolated sin. A long chain of events led me to choose death. I have compared my heart to that of David and found that my God has been as gracious to me as He was to David thousands of years before. The beauty of His heart has caused me to give Him mine.

The story of David's sin is recorded in 2 Samuel 11. Are you willing to compare some of the events of David's sin to your abortion experience for the sake of cleansing? If so, turn in your Bible to 2 Samuel 11 and begin by reading the entire chapter. Then answer the questions below.

5. Verse 1: "It happened in the spring of the year, at the time when kings go out to battle,... but David remained at Jerusalem." David was King of Israel, but he was not positioned in the right place at the right time. Think back to how you were positioned at the time of your pregnancy. How can a pregnancy be a good thing, but not at the right time?

   When is the right time for a baby to be conceived?

   Who has the power to make that choice?

6. We can only speculate as to why David did not go out to battle. He was a great national leader with military and political success and he was much loved by the people,. Is it possible that he grew arrogant through his success and became less dependent on God?

   In your abortion experience, were you depending on God, or on your own ability to control the situation?

7. Please read verses 3_4. If the king sends for you, you do not refuse him. David was a man of means and power. He abused that power to insist that Bathsheba sleep with him. At the time of your pregnancy, did anyone abuse you or betray your trust in their authority?

   Was there anyone less powerful than you that you abused?

8. Please read verses 5–6. This is the beginning of David's attempt to hide his sin. He is involving the commander of his army in this cover-up. Was there anyone in your abortion experience who became an accomplice with you? If so, how do you think the abortion has affected them?

9. Please read verses 7–13. This is an account of a tangled web of deception through repeated attempts to get Uriah to think that the child his wife was carrying was his own. Do you remember that God promised David that his seed would sit on the throne of Israel forever? Denying the child's identity would have denied him his inheritance.

   Think for a moment about your child's identity. In what ways did you deny his identity? If there are any additional issues you would like to confess and receive forgiveness for, please write your prayer in your journal today. Allow God to do a deep cleansing and bring purity to your motherhood.

10. When David's attempts at deception failed, he hoped to cover his sin with Bathsheba by murdering Uriah; he felt he had taken care of his problem and gotten away with everything. What is the last sentence of chapter 11?

    How did you feel immediately after your abortion?

11. Most of his life, David was in a different place spiritually than he was when he committed his sin with Bathsheba. Yet he came back to God with all His heart, and God did forgive him. He did not take away His inheritance, and He won't take away yours. After David confessed his sin in Psalm 51, he asked God for several things. List the things in each of the following verses that David wanted from God besides forgiveness.

    verse 10

    verse 11

    verse 12

    Can you honestly make this your prayer?

12. Understanding where you were spiritually when you chose abortion may help you to accept God's forgiveness. If you were not a believer when

you chose abortion, which of the following verses help you understand the reasons for your choice?

John 8:42–45

Ephesians 4:17–18

Colossians 1:21

Titus 3:3

13. If you were a believer at the time of your abortion, how do the following verses help you understand your reasons for choosing abortion even while confessing to know God?

Isaiah 29:13

Jeremiah 7:21-24

Romans 7:18

I Peter 5:8–9

My Journal

Power in the Blood — Day 2

In Old Testament times God instructed His people to make sacrificial offerings for forgiveness. He required them to name the specific transgression that was committed, and to make restitution wherever possible. Parts of those instructions are found in Leviticus 17. Please read verse 11in this chapter and answer these two questions:

1. What is in the blood? ____________________

2. Why did God give it to us upon the altar? __________________________

Everything about abortion is related to death and lies. The gospel is truth and life. God, the life source, created man for relationship with Him. When that relationship was broken through the disobedience of the first human, sin entered into the human race through Adam's blood. The price of sin is death, but price of life is in the blood. When God sent His Son, Jesus, He became the sacrifice for all our sins. It is through His Blood that we have forgiveness and eternal life. Did you ever wonder *why* His blood is so powerful?

A child's blood type comes from a chromosome from his mother's egg combined with a chromosome from his father's sperm. The virgin mother of Jesus conceived a child by Holy Spirit. That means that the blood of Jesus actually is the blood of His *heavenly* father and His *earthly* mother. When Jesus gave His life on the cross, He was able to represent the entire human race because his mother's egg made him fully human. The bloodline of His Father is divine, holy and pure. Bloodshed that does not have the divine nature of the Father would be a blemished unacceptable sacrifice, and it would not have the same effect. Jesus was a perfect sacrifice without blemish.

Read Matthew 27:50-53. Do you see the power of Jesus' blood to bring life out of the grave? There was so much life in Jesus' blood, that at the very moment of His death, bodies were raised out of their tombs. The Bible calls these people saints. That simply means that they had put their trust in God as the only one who could save them. It is this trust that sanctified them. When Jesus' blood was actually spilled, they received the power of life.

Long before Jesus came to the earth, God established covenant with those who trusted in Him. Covenant is an agreement with no expiration date. Covenant is a fusing of two beings— the two becoming one, as in a marriage. Covenant is established and sealed through the shedding of blood.

3 Read John 1:1, and then verse 14. Who is the Word? __________

God's divine plan was to provide Himself, His own blood, to pay the penalty (death) for sin. Jesus is called God's Son because He was reproduced by the Father. This is a divine mystery spoken of in Ephesians 3:9. God made Himself into a human being to come to earth to provide justice for our transgressions. It always amazes me that He decided to come the natural way – through childbirth. Jesus is the gospel. He is the good news that our sins are forgiven. He preached the gospel with His life, and He began preaching it by showing us the impact that a single preborn baby can have on the whole world.

When Jesus was circumcised on the eighth day of His life on earth, He shed holy blood to seal the covenant between God and man. When He prayed in the garden the night of His arrest, He sweat drops of holy blood. When He was arrested and beaten with a whip that ripped the meat from His back, He shed holy blood. When they tore His beard from His face, He shed holy blood. When He lay down and willingly stretched out His arms, the spikes punctured His wrists and they shed holy blood. When the soldiers crossed His feet and drove a spike through both ankles, He shed holy blood. When they pierced His side and water and blood gushed forth, it was holy, sinless blood.!

David said, "Behold, I was brought forth in iniquity, and in sin my mother conceived me." (Ps 51:5) Human beings all have a sinful nature. We are not born innocent because sin entered our blood line through Adam. Even if you and I could shed our own blood for someone, it would not save them, because our blood is not holy.

Jesus' loving sacrifice was more than an act meant to inspire us and impress us. He was not simply trying to create a new religion. A work needed to be done in order to free us from our debt to God. He finished that work.

I hurt God with my sin. I broke His heart. I needed to make amends so that we could have a relationship again. To atone for something is to try to make amends for it.

Many women try to atone for their abortions by having another baby soon after their abortion. A woman may sense the selfishness of her abortion, and want to prove to herself and to God that she is willing to be a mother. Other women become super-moms, always demanding perfection from themselves and their children. They cannot enjoy the present because of the weight of their past. The atonement in Jesus' blood satisfied all the requirements of God's law. Atonement wins back God's favor and His good will!

4 Read the following verses to see how the Blood of Jesus' sacrifice is related to atonement for our sins.

Exodus 30:10

Romans 3:25, 26

Colossians 2:14–15

Hebrews 2:17

5 How do you think lingering guilt has affected the choices you have made as a mother to your living children?

6 According to Romans 3:23-25 what is the only way our sins can be atoned for?

7 According to God's plan, how are sins forgiven?

Ephesians 2:8

Titus 3:5

8 Are you still trying to atone for your sins? What are some of the ways you have tried to work for your forgiveness?

9 Read Isaiah 53: 4-10 Then try to recount from memory some of the things that the prophet said Jesus would suffer for us.

Now please read verse 10 again. What do you think he meant by "When you make His soul and offering for sin, He shall prolong His days?" *Hint: Jesus is the one who was offering His soul for sin.*

God sent His Son to die so that I would not have to pay the price for having killed mine. Added to the torture He suffered through His trials and crucifixion was every disease and every vile and filthy sin. Every mocking and tormenting spirit attacked Him while He hung there until He breathed His last breath. All this He did for us!

After He has done all this for us, beloved, who are we to still say that we cannot forgive ourselves? God is the one who set the requirement for forgiveness, not us. When we say we cannot forgive ourselves, what we really mean is that there is still something we need to do. We are telling Jesus that what He did was not enough. What we really need to do is respect His plan and respect His sacrifice. We need to give honor and value to the payment that He made, and celebrate the power of His blood.

My Journal

Justice served — Day 3

Against You, You only, have I sinned, and done this evil in Your sight-That You may be found just when You speak, and blameless when You judge. Psalm 51: 4

The Old Covenant animal sacrifices were required to serve justice. The justice of God requires a penalty for sin. That penalty is death. Only blood can provide the restitution necessary to restore life. The elaborate sacrificial system of the blood of sheep and goats was a picture that God painted for His people. Thousands of years later His Son would be recognized as the Lamb of God, who takes away the sins of the world. The perfect mercy of God provided the payment for sin— the perfect sacrifice. His perfect love is demonstrated through His perfect justice.

God is the law-maker. He is also the chief executive and the supreme judge. He is the One who has set the boundaries of what is good and right, and He is the enforcer. When we cross those boundaries, we crossed Him. I cannot forgive my own sins against God. He is the only one who can forgive sins *against Himself.*

1. What truths about God and the forgiveness He extends to us are revealed in the following verses?

   Psalm 103:1–3

   Micah 7:18–19

2. Who can receive God's forgiveness?

   Acts 3:19

   Acts 10:43

   Isaiah 59:20

   God is a forgiving God, but forgiveness is not just His attitude toward us. Forgiveness is a price that has been paid for our wrongs. When we have looked closely at the sin of the abortion experience, we are left holding the bag. A wrong has been done. Someone has to pay.

3. Romans 6:23 says that there is a value placed on sin. What do we earn from sin? _______________To whom is our debt owed? ______________________

4. Please read Hebrews 9:28 When Jesus took all of our sin to the cross, who got paid?

5. What does God do when we confess our sins?

   Psalm 32:5

   Psalm 65:3

   Psalm 86:5

6. Are there any unconfessed sins that you would like to bring to God now? Write them in your journal page for today.

7. According to 1 John 1:9 what is God faithful to do if we confess our sin?

8. Why does 1 John 1: 9 say that God is "just" to forgive us, if we are guilty?

9. How was "justice" served for our sin of abortion?

My Journal

Provisions of His blood — Day 4

The thief does not come except to steal, and to kill, and to destroy.
I have come that they may have life,
and that they may have it more abundantly. John 10:10

John 10:10 speaks of the enemy of life itself. My agreement with abortion was collusion with a killer and bondage to his cruel government. The emotions and behaviors that followed were because of that bondage. The enemy was governing my mental health. The very reason that Jesus came to the earth was to rescue us from that bondage and bring us into a Kingdom of life.

1. Now read these two scriptures to see why Jesus came to the earth.

   1 John 3:8

   Hebrews 2:14

2. Now read Ephesians 4:8-10 to find out what happened right after Jesus died on the cross. Write what God shows you.

   When Jesus shed His blood, He went from the cross to the graves where human beings had been held captive. He descended into hell so we would not have to. Then He miraculously ascended to His Father to present His holy blood to be applied to our debt. I can see Him now, saying, "Father, Rhonda is being held captive by Satan to do his will. She is in bondage through her agreement with death. Father, I have paid the life of my blood to redeem her. Here is My Blood as payment to buy her freedom."

   To redeem something is to get or buy back, or reclaim something that was previously owned. In other words, our Father wanted to recover possession of us as a member of His family. We were purchased back from Satan's hold on us by the shed blood of Jesus.

3. Jesus' Blood provided redemption. As you read each of the following verses, fill in the blanks for a greater revelation of the provision of His blood.

   Ephesians 1: 7 We have redemption through His ____________________

   Galatians 4:4,5 God sent forth His son to ____________________ those who were under the law of sin and death.

   Colossians 1:14 Redemption is through the __________________________

   1 Peter 1: 18, 19 Know that you were redeemed with _________________

4. Jesus' Blood provided justification! Justice demands justification. If a crime is committed, there must be punishment in order to satisfy justice. Jesus did our time in prison for us. He was even executed for us. We are no longer sinners in the hands of an angry God. We are saints in the hands of a merciful and loving God. There is nothing more we must do to win favor with God or make up for our sin of abortion, sexual immorality, or any other sin.

   When we are justified, it is....**Just** as **if I'd** never done it!

   Please read these scriptures to understand the effects of justification, and fill in the blanks.

   Romans 5: 8--9 Since we have been justified by His ______________, God is not mad at us anymore. There is no reason to punish us.

   Romans 3: 24–25 When we were bought back from the adversary (redeemed), we were freely __________________. All justice was satisfied.

5. His blood provided reconciliation to the Father. We made ourselves His enemy by joining up with the devil's gang. We were fighting and feuding with God, but now the war is over. We have kissed and made up. He wants us and has taken us back. We have restored our friendship with God and we are in harmony in our relationship with Him.

   Colossians 1:20–21 It is God's pleasure to ______________________ us to Himself through the ____________________ of His cross.

   2 Corinthians 5:18 Says that it is through ______________________ that we are reconciled to God.

6. Jesus' Blood sanctified us. To sanctify something is to purify it, preparing it for sacred use. It can be compared to sterilizing a baby bottle, and then setting it in a special place to be used only to feed the baby. We've been cleansed and set apart to holiness. We are vessels prepared for His sacred use by our Father. Please read and understand the following scriptures about the provision of sanctification, and fill in the blanks.

   1 John 1:7 Says that the __________________ of Jesus is what cleanses us. Notice that the verb *cleanses* is ongoing. It started on the day you accepted His blood as payment for your sin, and it continues to this day.

   Hebrews 13:12 Jesus suffered for the in order to _____________________ the people with His _________________________ .

7. His blood provided acceptance. Unconditional love and acceptance is one of the most basic needs of all humanity. No matter how unacceptable the sin, God graciously accepts the repentant sinner. The very goal of His plan of salvation is to accept us back into His loving arms.

Ephesians 1: 4-6 God's plan is to make us ______________ in the Beloved

Ephesians 2:13 We are _________________ to God by the blood of Jesus.

8. The blood restored peace with God. The blood established a bond of peace with those who received this provision by faith. Do you seek peace? Read and meditate on these scriptures.

   Hebrews 13:20 Says that peace was established through the ____________ of an everlasting covenant. Jesus' blood was shed to cut a covenant between you and God that you may be at peace with him throughout eternity.

   John 14: 27 Jesus said, "My ________________ I give to you." We cannot manufacture peace. We get it through our covenant relationship with Jesus.

   Romans 15:13 We are filled with this peace by ____________________

   Isaiah 54:10 God promises that His ____________________ of peace shall not be removed from you.

My Journal

Cleansing the conscience **Day 5**

Hebrews 9:14 says that the blood of Jesus is able to cleanse our conscience of works that lead to death so that we can be free to serve the living God. Our past lifestyle led to the death of our child. The blood of Jesus not only forgave us, but also cleansed our conscience so that we can be free from our past. We can now make life-affirming choices without trying to make up for the past.

Can you say, "I am forgiven," with confidence? Further assurances of God's love and forgiveness can be found in Psalm 103. Rewrite each verse to state either "I am forgiven because..." or "I am loved because..." for example, verse 3 could be rewritten, "I am forgiven because he forgives all my sins."

Verse 4

Verse 5

Verse 8

Verse 9

Verse 10

Verse 11

1. How far from you has he removed your sins? Psalm 103:12

7. What does God do after he forgives all your sins? Isaiah 43: 25

Are you waiting to "feel" forgiven or are you walking in forgiveness based on your trust in the blood of Jesus? Forgiveness is not something based on feelings. Once forgiven, "feeling" guilty is believing a lie. The emotion that you feel is unworthiness. The lie is "I'm not good enough to be forgiven" or "I don't deserve to be forgiven."

When I was first married, my husband and I wanted a house to raise our children in. I had messed up my credit and I was unworthy of a loan. My husband was an immigrant with no citizenship. We could not qualify for a loan. We purchased the house in his sister's name. Her good name was a gift to us. Today the home is in our name and we have it as an inheritance for our children. God wants you to accept forgiveness as a gift in the name of His Son. He wants you to be empowered by the gift of a clean conscience so that you can have an inheritance in Him.

1. *Read Colossians 1:12 to see who qualified you for an inheritance.*
2. Do you feel condemnation for your past sins? If so, what must you do to be free from condemnation? Rom. 8:1–4

Sometimes we hold on to our guilt because we have become accustomed to being defective. It is easier to be lost and depressed than to take responsibility for walking in the truth.

3. Wanting to punish yourself is saying to God that the sacrifice of his Son was not enough to cover you sins. Is there anything you have been denying yourself because of your abortion? Are there any ways you have been punishing yourself? Is there anything else God could have done to cover your sins?

My Journal

OFFENDER **OFFENSES**

1. ____

2. ____

3. ____

4. ____

5. ____

6. ____

7. ____

8. ____

9. ____

10. ____

11. ____

12. ____

List each person that you need to forgive and each offense that must be forgiven.
Please be as specific as you can about the way that they have offended and hurt you.

Forgiving Others

Session 8

So My heavenly Father will also do to you if each of you, from his heart, does not forgive his bother his trespasses. Matthew 18:35

When we come to fully understand how much we need forgiveness, and experience the joy that comes from being set free, we have a new grace to forgive others. This week we will be studying scripture to see why we should forgive and how we can forgive others. My prayer is that you will see the benefits of forgiving others and make your decision to forgive a daily way of life.

Forgive from the heart — Day 1

Forgiving others does not come easy. When we are hurt everything inside us wants to give hurt back. The first step in forgiving is being honest about how you have been hurt. Please allow God to heal your hurts by listing those who have offended you on your **Offender / Offenses Worksheet.** Beside each name, write specifically how they hurt you. There may be more than one offense for each person who offended you.

God is the Almighty Judge. He is the standard of right and wrong. He is the only one who can forgive people's sins against Him. He judges the motives of the heart. We do not know people's heart. God can refuse to forgive those whose hearts have rejected Him because He is God. We're not. We can choose to share God's forgiveness that was bought with Jesus' Blood. We cannot refuse anyone God's forgiveness. It belongs to Him, and He has extended it to sinners throughout His creation.

1. Read the parable in Matthew 18:21–35 and apply it to your abortion experience by putting yourself in the place of the unforgiving servant. Your master is God, and your fellow servant is someone from your abortion experience whom you have been unable to forgive.

   From what debt has your master released you?

In verses 29 and 30, how did the servant treat his fellow servant?

What characteristic of Jesus (verse 33) are we to display when forgiving others?

According to verse 35, from where must our forgiveness come?

2. Who is the person in your experience that it is hardest to forgive? Why?

3. Name some of the reasons that it can be difficult to forgive others.

   One reason it is difficult to forgive others is that they are **not sorry** for what they have done. It does not seem just to let them off the hook when there is no change of heart. You may feel you have a right to set up conditions before you will forgive someone for his or her part in the abortion. You may want the person to show remorse or to confess guilt before you will forgive them.

4. To help in determining if you are resisting forgiving others, finish these statements, inserting the person(s) you listed in question number 2 who are most difficult to forgive.

   I will forgive ________________________ if....

   I will forgive ________________________ if....

   I will forgive ________________________ if....

   I will forgive ________________________ if....

5. According to Luke 17:3–4, what is the condition for forgiveness?

6. Are you still required to forgive if others even if they have hurt you many times without being sorry? Mark 11:25–26

7. If your abortion was a pregnancy that resulted from sexual abuse; are you willing to forgive the perpetrator for abusing you?

8. If you know that someone has something against you, are you to wait until he or she comes to you for forgiveness? Matthew 5:23–24

9. Read John 20:22 – 23 carefully. What gift did Jesus give His disciples before He gave this instruction?

   Are you willing to ask Him for the power of the Holy Spirit to help you forgive?

   What happens to the sins of those we do not forgive?

   If they sincerely ask God to forgive them, do you think He will?

   What if this happens and you know nothing about it?

   According to the above scripture, who will retain the sin?

10. In each of these Scriptures, record the person who was able to forgive others *before* seeing signs of repentance.

    Acts 7:59–60

    2 Timothy 4:16–17

    Luke 23:34

11. What or who do you think Stephen, Paul, and Jesus trusted in the above scripture passages?

12. Have the people in your abortion experience asked you to forgive them for the ways they have hurt you?

    Are you willing to forgive them even if they never asked you to?

    What will you have to trust God for in order to forgive each of them from the heart?

    In order to forgive ____________, I will have to trust God for _________.

    In order to forgive ____________, I will have to trust God for _________.

In order to forgive ____________, I will have to trust God for _________.

In order to forgive ____________, I will have to trust God for _________.

In order to forgive ____________, I will have to trust God for _________.

In order to forgive ____________, I will have to trust God for _________.

In order to forgive ____________, I will have to trust God for _________.

Perhaps one of the ways that others have hurt you is that they have destroyed your trust. This is especially true in the case of a sexual perpetrator or an authority figure who coerced you into having the abortion.

Without trust you will not be able to build healthy relationships. This does not mean that you have to trust everyone. It means that you must renew your trust in God. He will give you the spiritual discernment to know where to set healthy boundaries. Then you will know who and how to trust.

13. In 1 Corinthians 12:10–11 there is a spiritual gift mentioned called discerning of spirits. This is a gift from God that will allow you to know when to place your trust. You must pray to receive it. Read the passage and see how to have the gift of discernment.

14. Romans 15:13 says that you will have peace as you put your trust in ______ and that you will overflow with hope by the power of the ________________.

15. Please re-read John 20:22– 23. By what power do you forgive men's sins?

My Journal

Forgiven much, loves much — Day 2

I am grateful that God Himself revealed to me the horror of abortion. In the same moment that He showed me a visual image in my mind of my son being torn apart in a late-term abortion, I felt a peace like anointing oil running from my head down my back.

He didn't make excuses for my sin. He showed me the depth of what I had been forgiven of. He showed me a picture of His grace by showing me the truth of what I'd done. I can appreciate God's mercy because I have looked at the damage that my sin caused to me and others. He is the one who has shown me all these things; yet He is the one who has forgiven me. Isn't His love amazing!

When I forgave my perpetrator for childhood sexual abuse, I was more than happy to extend that same grace to him. I had much love for him; because I knew that I had been forgiven much by the One I hurt.

1. Read Luke 7:36–50. For what was this woman forgiven in verses 47–48?

2. What was the result of her being forgiven in verse 50?

   Peace Floods your soul when you have been forgiven. So it is when we forgive others. We replace the anger and hate in our hearts with love and peace toward our brothers and sisters.

3. How are we to treat those who have hurt us?

   Luke 6:27–28

   1 Peter 3:9

4. If we choose to love each other, what happens in our relationship with God?

   1 John 4:12

   When we forgive others, we witness to the world Christ's forgiveness in this world. The more someone has hurt you, the greater your witness of love to them will be. Christ died for all those who have hurt you in the past, those who are hurting you now, and those who will hurt you in the future. Consider the offenses of others an opportunity to glorify Him!

   God wants us to forgive because He has forgiven us. He wants us to show mercy to others because He has shown us His mercy. Mercy means no longer hoping in our hearts that they get what they deserve, no longer wanting to see them punished.

   and write your prayer on the journal page for today.

My Journal

Sowing and Reaping — Day 3

The Bible teaches us not to judge or we will be judged in the same way we judge others. We can choose to release from our judgment those who have hurt us and choose instead to have mercy on them. In releasing others from our prideful judgment, we in turn are released from the bondage of unforgiveness.

What does it mean to judge someone? The dictionary definition of JUDGE:

1. To form an opinion about through careful weighing of evidence and testing of premises.

2. to determine or pronounce after inquiry and deliberation.

3. to decide or form an opinion about someone. Remember that we are to use good judgment about things, but not to form opinions about a person.

1. What are the results of showing mercy to others?

   Luke 6:35–36

2. What are the consequences of not showing mercy to others? James 2:13

   Why do you think the above verse says that "mercy triumphs over judgment"?

3. Why are we not to judge our brothers and sisters?

   Romans 14:10–12

   2 Corinthians 5:10

4. How will we be judged if we judge others? Matthew 7:1–2

5. Matthew 7:3–5 refers to a type of spiritual blindness.

   How can we begin to see clearly?

6. Judgment can be a plank in our own eye. It is a bad seed. When we sow it, comes back to us. Creator God has a law in the universe that some call the "Law of reciprocity". It is found in Galatians 6:7. Exactly what can we expect?

7. In Matthew 7, the Lord tells us about judgment coming back to us, or reaping what we sow. Do not think of the measure that you use as only being used once upon you. The measure of judgment is rather, the type of judgment that you heap upon others. For example, when you judge others to be stupid, you will be seen as stupid.

   Spiritual principals are just like things that God made in the natural. If judgment is a seed we sow, then it will come back to us like a seed. If I sow a tomato seed, what I will probably get is a tomato plant. It will then produce fruit, and the fruit will be loaded with like seeds.

8. What kind of results come from sowing in these two verses?

   Matthew 13:32

   Hosea 8:7

My Journal

Bitter Root Judgments **Day 4**

Think for a moment about some of the relationships that were important to you, but they fell apart. Where there are patterns of broken relationships, there is probably a root of judgment that was sown against you or by you. Ask the LORD to show you if there was a seed of judgment sown. Write what He shows you here.

1. Forgiveness is not complete without release from judgment. You must pray to release the people you listed at the beginning of today's lesson from your judgment. Pray like this for each one:

   "Father, in the Name of Jesus, I release my judgments against *name of the person* for *specific way in which you judged them.*

2. Forgiveness is a type of giving. It is extending the same gift that we were given by Jesus to others. How does Luke 6:38 say you will be repaid for this gift?

   As you forgive, ask God to forgive *you* for judging the person.

3. As we learned in Lesson 3, we have the God-given power and authority to break a curse in our life. Matt 5:44 tells us how to keep from reaping the curse of judgment. What must you do?

4. Jesus showed us this power in Matthew 21:18-21. What happened to the seed of that fig tree?

5. Are you ready to break the power of reaping seeds of judgments that you have sown? Pray this prayer for every judgment God has and will show you:

   "Father, I now break the power of reaping *type of judgment* and the curse that has been released upon me as a result of my judging *person judged.*"

6. In Matthew 27:52 we see that the Blood of Jesus had the power to open graves and raise the dead. Apply this power in your covenant relationship to these bitter root judgments. "I now bring the power of the Blood of Jesus to bear upon these bitter root judgments. I break their power over me, in Jesus' Name."

My Journal

Ignorance is not bliss — Day 5

1. Look back to the section where you set up conditions for forgiveness. In Luke 23:34, Jesus says, "Heavenly Father, forgive them for ....

2. Read Ephesians4:18. Not knowing what they are doing is the kind of ignorance spoken of in this verse. We do not justify people's sin by ignorance. They are still guilty. We forgive them even though they are guilty; as God is Christ forgave us even though we were guilty. God did not make an excuse for our sin. He made a remedy. It was only His Blood that justified our sin.

3. Forgiving someone because they didn't know is not an excuse. It is an attitude of understanding that we are all spiritually blind in some ways. You can rest assured that when we get to heaven, we will suddenly see a lot of things that we didn't see before. Read 2 Corinthians 3:18.

4. Thank God, He chose to forgive us before we saw everything we needed to repent of. You can choose to be like Him today. You can say over each of the people on your list:

   "Dear God, I forgive ______ for He/she did not know what he/she was doing."

   "Dear God, I forgive ______ for He/she did not know what he/she was doing."

   "Dear God, I forgive ______ for He/she did not know what he/she was doing."

   "Dear God, I forgive ______ for He/she did not know what he/she was doing."

   "Dear God, I forgive ______ for He/she did not know what he/she was doing."

5. Many times we are so focused on how others have hurt us, we don't even see how we have hurt them. Have you asked God to forgive you for the ways you have unknowingly hurt others? Stop now and write your prayer asking God for forgiveness on your journal page for today.

6. We are going to do a powerful exercise in class to cleanse us of all unforgiveneness and bitterness and judgment. Once you have been cleansed of all roots of bitterness, you must examine your heart daily to be sure that no bitterness is returning.

   Psalm 4:4

   Psalm 139:23–24

7. Will God hear your prayers if you have unforgiveness in your heart?

   1 Peter 3:10–12

8. Read Jeremiah 1:10 to see what God told this prophet he must do before He could build and plant. Spend time with God, asking Him where you have allowed bitterness and judgment to take root in your heart. You have the tools within this lesson to purge yourself of these roots. May He rest upon you and give you peace. Pray this prayer with me:

   "Lord, cleanse these areas of my heart and make me free to love with a pure heart."

9. If we have strongholds of judgment or unforgiveness in our lives, we will pass this curse to our children as we spend time parenting them. If we are calling upon God with a pure heart, our children will learn our ways from us and be blessed. Read Isaiah 61:9. What will others do when they see the way our children live?

My Journal

To Know You is To Love You

Session 9

Everyone who loves is born of God and knows God. 1 John 4:7

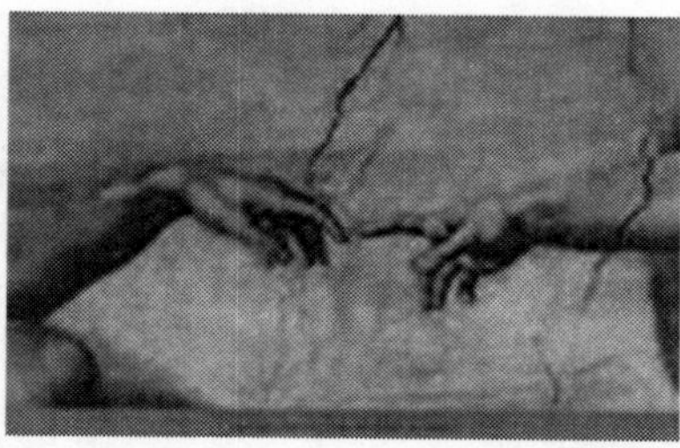

God is relational. Father, Son and Holy Spirit were relational before man was ever created. The Trinity is the essence of a perfect harmonious relationship. The Father could have performed all the functions of the Son and of Holy Spirit without being the three-Gods-in-one, but He chose to base everything in all of creation on this one attribute of His character. He started with relationship. Everything that He created has a relationship to the rest of His creation. We are in some kind of relationship with everything around us. The freewill acceptance of this interdependence on one another is love.

Have you ever heard, "There's no love like a mother's love?" The truth of this statement lies in the fact that the mother/child relationships starts out in utter interdependence. The unborn baby is dependent on the mother for its very survival. The mother is somewhat dependant on the child on a higher level. Her relationship to the child will affect her fulfillment of purpose. A mother's purpose is integrally linked to her child's destiny. She is the nurturer of that destiny, and unless she fulfills her purpose, the child's destiny cannot come to pass.

At the time of my abortion, I was not willing to have a relationship the child in my womb. I denied myself the privilege of knowing a mother's love. Raising subsequent children, I came to understand love by knowing my children. As my relationship grew in intimacy with them, my capacity to love grew. An important part of my restoration has been to get to know my children – all of them, both the living and those that have gone on to heaven. My aborted children are now in a closer relationship with God than we can know here on earth. They are living forever with God. They still exist, and I still want to know them.

In the Image of God Day 1

The abounding love of the Trinity overflowed and demanded to reproduce itself. Then God spoke to Himself and proclaimed, "Let Us make man in our image," but what did He mean by "in Our Image"? One definition of *image* is a 'representation of a person or thing'. We are here on the earth to re-present God and His love to the world.

1. Who does Colossians 1:15 say is the image of God?
2. What did Jesus say about His representation of God in John 14:7?

   It is very difficult to know someone you have never seen. Jesus was the first visual representation of God in human terms. We could see Him. God was drawing us into closer relationship by giving us an understandable image of Himself. Most people still relate to this part of the Trinity more than the other two. Perhaps this has to do with the fact that long after His resurrection, there are still images of Jesus everywhere.

   As mothers of aborted children, we have a special dependence on the Holy Spirit to remember our children. We have never seen a visual image of them with our natural eyes. But this lack of natural experience does not have to remain a handicap in knowing who they are and restoring our mother's love for them.

   After Jesus was resurrected, He was not known by His disciples on the road to Emmaus. (Luke 24:13–32) Still, there was a knowing that they sensed while they were with Him. They stated "Did not our hearts burn within us while we walked along the road and while He opened the Scriptures (concerning Himself) to us?" They were visually handicapped, but when He talked about Himself through the scriptures, their spiritual eyes were opened.

   This kind of spiritual enlightenment about who your child is can make your heart burn within you. I encourage you to fall in love with your child by getting to know him or her through the Spirit of the eternal living God. Take courage in facing the fact that your child is alive in heaven with God, that God knows all things about this child He created, and that He is willing to show you who he or she is.

3. Spiritual existence in eternity is beyond our present comprehension. Please read 1 Corinthians 15:42 to see what we do know about the bodies that exist in heaven.

   When we get to heaven, we will know our children by their spirit. In Matthew 17 Moses and Elijah appeared to Peter, James, and John with Jesus. These guys had been dead a long time, and they were not raised from the dead. The disciples had never seen a photograph of Moses or Elijah, yet they knew them immediately and called them by name.

4. What does Jesus say in verse 9? "Tell the ________________ to no one until the Son of Man is risen from the dead." The Lord was giving them spiritual __________________ to see into the eternal spiritual world.

   God wants to do that for us, too. He wants to give us a relative, relational image of our children so that we can know them, understand them, and restore our love for them. It's important that we have this now, and not wait until we get to heaven. The more our love is restored, the more capable of loving and receiving love we will be on earth. This glorifies God, for we are here to re-present Him, and God is love.

5. Read Matthew 19:4. If we are to know the image of the child whom God made, one of the first things we may want to ask of Him is, "Is my child a boy or a girl?' Will you go to the Creator of your child now and ask of Him? Begin this journey of getting to know and love your child by finding out if he is a boy or she is a girl. Write what He shows you.

My Journal

In the Name **Day 2**

Have you ever thought about what it means to say, "In the Name of Jesus"? We are assigning the character and integrity of His Name to what we are speaking. We are invoking the authority of His good Name. But what does His Name actually mean?

1. Jesus' parents named Him. But where did they get the Name? What does the name Jesus mean? Read Matthew 1:21 for the answers.
2. Read Matthew 1:23 to find another name for Jesus and what it meant.

   What we call someone or something is a powerful indicator of whom or what it is or will become. When God spoke all of creation into existence, it became what He called it. Adam's first job was to name the rest of God's Creation. As someone who shared in the dominion of God's planet, Adam was to assign a character to the animals by giving them an appropriate name. Throughout the Bible, a person or place was given a name because of something that happened there, or because of circumstances of a person's birth or a prophesy about his destiny. When we give our child a name, we are acknowledging the existence of a person with the character and personality appropriate to that name.

   A parent's job is to nurture our children's God-given purpose. We can speak what God has ordained for them. This goes for our aborted children as well, since we are still their parents. Even though they have gone on, we can honor their purpose on the earth by naming them, and speaking their name to others.

   Following is a list of names and their meanings. You may be able to find more in the unit library. Prayerfully consider the name that you want to give your child. In our memorial service next session, you will be given a certificate of life much like the one you would get in a hospital had you birthed the baby there. You will have the opportunity to publically acknowledge your child by name and celebrate his/her personality.

My child's name is ____

Because he/she ____

____

____

____

Boys' Names

Adam – a man of the red earth

Brian – strong; sincere

Caleb – bold

David – beloved

Eric – princely

Frederick – peaceful ruler

Geoffrey – brave

Harrison – noble; princely

Isaiah – God is my helper

John - God is gracious

Kenneth – handsome

Leif – beloved

Matthew – gift of the Lord

Nathan – gift

Oswald – power of God

Peter – reliable, dependable, a rock

Quinn – the wise

Ray – kingly

Stephen – loyal

Theodore – gift of God

Uriah – the Lord is my light

Victor – conquering

Warren – protecting friend

Xavier – brilliant

Yates – dweller by the gates

Zachary – Jehovah hath remembered.

Girls' Names

Abigail – joy of the Father

Beatrice – blessing

Candace – glowing

Dorothy – God's gift

Elizabeth – promise of God

Eve - Out of man

Faith – sure reliance

Gloria – the glorious

Hannah – good

Ina – pure

Jane God's grace

Kim – Chief, ruler

Libby – consecrated to God

Louise – famous in battle

Melissa – Honeybee

Minna – loving memory

Naomi – sweet, pleasant

Olivia – bringer of peace

Priscilla – dutiful, lovely

Rebecca – peacemaker

Sophia – wise

Shaina – beautiful

Theresa - harvester

Xenia – hospitable

Yvette – The archer

Zoe – flight, freedom

How Will My Baby Relate to Me? Day 3

The thought of meeting your baby in heaven can be a scary one if you have unanswered questions. We sometimes think of our children plagued with many questions, and frustrated with our choice of abortion. Some mothers may think of what her defense will be when she meets her child. She may want to try to explain herself.

Please rest assured that God has planned a glorious homecoming for you and a beautiful reunion with your child in heaven. Please allow the truth of these scriptures to put your heart at peace.

1. Is there a place for me in heaven? (John 14:3)
2. Is my child sad when he/she thinks of me? (Rev 21:4)
3. How can my child ever forgive me for what I did to her/him? What does Matthew 6:14–15 say about all those who are now residing in heaven?
4. Will my child have questions about why I chose abortion over life for him or her? Please read 1 Corinthians 13:12 to see what those who are face to face with God in heaven know.

As you meditate on these scriptures, please allow Holy Spirit to show you what your reunion with your child in heaven will be like. Write what He shows you in your journal for today.

My Journal

Created to be Creative — Day 4

If we have been created in the very image of the Great Creator, what is the possibility of us not being creative? There is a talent and a creative gift in every human being. 1 Peter 1:3 says that His divine nature has been imparted to us to give us everything we need for LIFE and godliness.

The memorial is a celebration of LIFE. It is a time to celebrate the fact that every human being that God created has value. The value of your creative talents will be celebrated as well. There will be a time for every mother to speak about her child and share what God has shown you, celebrating what you have come to know and appreciate about your baby. During this time you may want to share a poem or a song. Perhaps you can say it better in a drawing or a dance. Some mothers just have a way of expressing themselves that make them very good speakers. Whatever your gift, use it to glorify God and honor your child during the coming memorial service.

Today continue preparing your heart to honor God and your child's life at the memorial service next session. Spend today thinking about what you want to say in the time you have to contribute to the memorial service.

My Journal

The Purpose of a Memorial — Day 5

Perhaps one of the fundamental reasons so many post-abortive women carry guilt and grief for so many years is because they have never had an opportunity to complete the natural death-related grieving process. When death occurs, normally, we have a funeral. This is not for the person who died, but for those who remain. It is a time of officially letting go, a time for closure so that you can move on to the glorious future that God has planned for you.

Because you never got to see your baby or hold him or her, you are left with empty, aching arms; a feeling that can seemingly never be completely filled. Have you ever had the desire to hold your baby and be close to him or her? The memorial service gives you an opportunity to acknowledge an enduring bond with your baby.

It is important for you to participate in the Memorial service in order to commit your baby into the hands of the One Who Gives Life – Jesus. No matter how a mother has lost her child, she needs to grieve that loss. Your guilt has been dealt with at the cross, and your heart and mind has been renewed. Now it is time to release the tears that have been held back and grieve the loss of your child apart from any guilt or shame.

The purpose of the memorial is for you to bring closure to your loss, but also to give honor to God as the Creator, and to your baby as an eternal being who deserves to be loved as a full-fledged member of your family.

My Journal

A Higher Life Calling

Session 10

He established a testimony in Jacob,... that they may set their hope in God, and not forget the works of God.Psalm 78:5a, 7a

Your history with God is the most solid foundation for truth that you will ever have. When you remember what God has done, you carry in your heart the praise of who He is. Remembering who He is will maintain and increase your intimacy with Him, and make His grace continually more accessible to you. It is this access by faith to His grace that will empower you to make choices that bring abundant life.

My prayer for you in this lesson is that you will have the tools necessary to walk in new life after abortion, and never again agree with death in any form.

Finding the redemptive purpose — Day 1

I trust that by now you are settled in your heart that God is a God of life, and that He will never ask us to take the life of a child He created as a gift to us. He did not plan your abortion. That happened by choice – a choice outside the will of God.

1. Romans 8:28 says, "And we know that all things work together for good to those who love God, to those who are called according to _______________ _______________________.

   This verse speaks of the *redemptive* purpose of God, in which He makes all things new. It is written by the apostle Paul in the context of the doctrine of salvation. He is teaching the church in Rome that they were not only saved *from* something, but were also saved *for* something.

2. In the apostle's letter of instruction to the saints at Philippi in Chapter 3, verse 12, he calls the saints to press on, that they may lay hold of the very thing that they were embraced by God _________.

3. Sister, even inside the isolation of a prison, you have an apostle who continually equips and establishes you for what you were saved *for*. Please read Hebrews 3:1 to find out who it is. Write His Name here in big letters.

   What we have been dealing with over the last 10 weeks is the truth about the sanctity of human life. This whole concept is based upon the fact that the Creator created every human being for a special purpose. Your ability to press on and reach your God-given purpose in life will of necessity involve staying connected to Him. He is the life source, and a continual *re-source*.

   Do you feel more connected to God than you did at the beginning of this journey?

   That connection will help you see the good purpose that God can work in your life in spite of the bad choices you have in the past. He has redeemed you for a purpose.

   There are good things that have been placed in your heart by your Creator. Trust that He wants to help you bring them to pass. What sort of things do you care about? What do you enjoy doing? What do you see yourself doing five or maybe ten years from now? There may be things in your dreams that you never dared to tell anyone about. In your newfound freedom, you will find yourself with more boldness. This is the boldness that comes from revelation of His love for every human being that He created. Today take a step toward your future by writing out the purpose that you feel God created you for in your journal page.

My Journal

Sharing with friends and family — Day 2

Remember the day you first got saved? If you were like me, you couldn't wait to tell someone. It was a truth so liberating, so wonderful, and so refreshing that the joy of it was too much to contain inside my own heart.

1. For some of us, we shared that joy with such vigor and vitality that we scared some people. We may have even experienced rejection by some. Read 1 Thessalonians 4:8 to understand who was really being rejected.

   God is the source of salvation. A source used over and over becomes a re-source. God is our salvation every day. Your renewal after abortion is a kind of life after death. It is really another salvation experience that you will likely want to share.

2. Read 1 Samuel 2:1 to see how Hannah, a woman who already knew God, responded to the Lord's salvation as a new life experience.

3. Are there any close friends or family members that you will want to share your abortion *recovery* experience with? How do you imagine that they will respond?

4. Please settle in your heart how you will respond to God's goodness, even if others do not. Do you believe that abortion is a good choice for some women? What are some of the reasons why a person may take that point of view?

   Some friends and family may try to comfort you with excuses for your abortion. They may try to think of why you "needed" to do it at the time.

   The problem with the pregnancy was not the baby; it was what you believed.

5. Please take the time to remember the major false belief that you had at the time of your abortion.

   Now write the truth that Holy Spirit has revealed to you regarding that false belief.

   Testifying is a choice. Remember that you do not have to share your testimony with anyone. You are being offered the privilege of doing so.

6. You also get to choose who you will share it with and in what context.

   What about those we hurt? The best witness we can give to them is an apology that speaks of our repentance. If there is something we have taken from them, can it be restored? To make restitution means to restore something to its rightful owner, or to its former state. The following Scriptures show examples of restitution. How is restitution made in each case?

Numbers 5:5–8 Try to apply this in terms of the New Covenant.

Ephesians 4:28

Luke 19:8

7. What is your major motivation for sharing your testimony?

   Some good reasons for sharing your testimony are:

   - To reveal God's grace in your life.
   - To reveal the character of God and His redemptive purposes.
   - To reveal God's truth about abortion to someone.
   - To help someone else make a choice that brings life instead of death.

   Some "not-so-good" reasons for sharing your testimony are:

   - To convince someone that abortion is wrong
   - To give someone an excuse for having an abortion
   - To test whether the person will reject you or not
   - To "get it off your chest"

Today spend some time deciding which of your family members or close friends you'd like to share your abortion recovery experience with. Be sure you are doing it for the right reasons, and pray about the right time and place to share with them. Write your thoughts in today's journal page.

My Journal

Sharing with your children — Day 3

1. Please read Psalm 78, verses 5– 7 and answer the following questions by reading the scriptures in order:

   Who established your testimony?

   Why did He establish it?

   What does He want our children to do with what they hear?

   Why does He want our grandchildren to know the testimony?

   One of the greatest motivations for keeping the testimony about how abortion affected us is to save our children and their children after them the heartache and pain. If our children are not sexually pure, they will be threatened by an unplanned pregnancy. There is no sure-fire contraceptive except abstinence. If they become pregnant, they will be faced with the choice of whether to have an abortion.

   Educating the next generation starts with the family. Our daughters need to know in advance that abortion is not the easy solution to an unplanned pregnancy that we hoped it would be. Knowing how abortion affected us can strengthen their resolve to remain abstinent until marriage. This is a decision that can save their hearts, their minds, and their bodies from much pain.

2. After considering whether to tell your children about your abortion, you might also consider when and how. If you are honest about your deception and fears at the time of the pregnancy, you will find that your children are very forgiving. If you try to make excuses, they will not trust your love for them.

   As a renewed mother, you will have your children's best interest in mind. Here are some things to consider for their benefit:

   - Tell them what they need to know. Don't be too forthcoming with details that are not relevant to their understanding. As in all communications with children about sexual matters, answer their questions as directly as you can without too much embellishment.

   - Never lie to your children. Trust will be a major issue surrounding the revelation of the abortion.

   - Are they developmentally ready? Consider how they have developed mentally. *Generally* speaking, younger than 8 is too young. Children begin to think conceptually and are best able to process things conceptually between the ages of 8 and 10. By that time, they should also have a concept of God and the afterlife that will be helpful in explaining where their siblings are.

- After you tell them, assure them of your love for them.
- Be aware that grief comes in delayed reactions. Be watchful in the days and weeks after you tell them if there are any mood swings. Initiate a dialogue if you see these changes. Periodically ask them how they feel about the abortion. Ask them if they have questions about what you talked about before and assure them that you are open to answering their questions. Don't drill them with yours.
- Pray with them after you tell them. Thank God for His mercy and grace and His care for the siblings who are in heaven.
- Play with them after you tell them. It is very important for them to have positive experiences with you after you have shared that you took the life of one of their siblings.
- Realize that they are dealing with a death experience. If there has been another loss of a loved one in the family that they have processed, consider making the analogy.

Today, please journal why you would or would not want to tell your children about your abortion experience and your recovery. Include when it would be appropriate for them to hear it and how you plan to present it to them.

My Journal

Pre-writing your testimony — Day 4

A testimony of Jesus glorifies God. A testimony of pain and degradation glorifies Satan. It's your testimony. You can choose who you want to get the glory.

You will be given some helpful tools for pre-writing your testimony. These are questionnaires designed to help you think through how abortion has affected you and what God has done to renew your mind and heal your emotions. After you have finished them, summarize what you have said by writing a shorter version of your story below.

Focus on what you know now that you wish you'd known before you made the abortion decision. Think of how the abortion most affected you, and how that symptom was healed through the study. Tell how God changed your thoughts and feelings about abortion.

You will be given time at the graduation class to share this one-minute testimony with the class. May you have a new testimony every day of His faithfulness to you.

My Story

God Calling **Day 5**

We cannot work for our forgiveness, but we are invited to co-labor with God **because** we have been forgiven Freedom from the effects of abortion means that we are now able to participate in our Father's business. Our blood-bought righteousness brings us in to union with a holy God, and we will love what He loves and abhor what he does. God is not requiring anything burdensome from us. He is calling us to a higher purpose than our own comforts.

1. Please read Micah 6:8 to see the simple requirements of our calling. Write these three things down here.
2. Please read Rev.1:5 to see what you have been set free from.
3. Now read the next verse, Rev.1:6 to see what the result of being washed in the blood is. What title does the Lord give to you?
4. What kind of authority does this give you in your present situation?

   You will never have real authority in the earth until you learn to steward the reality of your spiritual authority. Now is the time to begin doing that. As you walk in union with your Creator every day, He will show you the next step to fulfillment of your own special calling.

   We can never physically replace the lives that were lost through abortion, but we can help restore some other lives. We can't bring our child back to earth, but we can honor his memory by not denying that he ever existed.

   We can now honor the sanctity of human life by fulfilling our own God-given purpose. We can truly surrender our lives to the One who gave us eternal life. We can allow our special gifts and talents to be used for God in the way He chooses. We can help other women who need our support and encouragement.

   Is there any way you would like to serve because you have been forgiven? Share it with God in your journal today, and consider sharing with others at graduation. In Revelation 2, the Lord calls even those who are in prison to be faithful until death, and He promises them a crown of life.

5. Now, please read Revelation 3:11 as final instruction to you.

   In His Unfailing Love, Rhonda Arias

My Journal

My Journal